Selected Poems

Other books by James Tate

The Lost Pilot

The Oblivion Ha-Ha

Hints to Pilgrims

Absences

Hottentot Ossuary

Viper Jazz

Riven Doggeries

Constant Defender

Reckoner

Distance from Loved Ones

James Tate

SELECTED

POEMS

WESLEYAN UNIVERSITY PRESS

Published by University Press of New England / Hanover & London

WESLEYAN UNIVERSITY PRESS
Published by University Press of New England, Hanover, NH 03755

© 1991 by James Tate

All rights reserved.

Printed in the United States of America   5   4   3   2   1
CIP data appear at the end of the book

The Lost Pilot, Yale University Press, 1967; Ecco Press, 1982; included by per-
mission of Ecco Press. *The Oblivion Ha-Ha,* Unicorn Press, 1970; included by
permission. *Hints to Pilgrims,* University of Massachusetts Press, 1971; included
by permission. *Absences,* Atlantic Monthly Press, 1972; Carnegie Mellon Univer-
sity Press, 1990. *Hottentot Ossuary,* Temple Bar Press, 1974. *Viper Jazz,* Wesleyan
University Press, 1976; included by permission. *River Doggeries,* Ecco Press,
1979; included by permission. *Constant Defender,* Ecco Press, 1983; included by
permission. *Reckoner,* Wesleyan University Press, 1986; included by permission.

Contents

III *from* Hints to Pilgrims (1971)

IV *from* Absences (1972)

V   *from* Hottentot Ossuary (1974)

VI   *from* Viper Jazz (1976)

IX *from* Reckoner (1986)

I

from The Lost Pilot

(1 9 6 7)

Manna

I do remember some things
times when I listened and heard
no one saying no, certain
miraculous provisions
of the much prayed for manna
and once a man, it was two
o'clock in the morning in
Pittsburg, Kansas, I finally
coming home from the loveliest
drunk of them all, a train chugged,
goddamn, struggled across a
prairie intersection and
a man from the caboose real-
ly waved, honestly, and said,
and said something like my name.

The Book of Lies

I'd like to have a word
with you. Could we be alone
for a minute? I have been lying
until now. Do you believe

I believe myself? Do you believe
yourself when you believe me? Lying
is natural. Forgive me. Could we be alone
forever? Forgive us all. The word

is my enemy. I have never been alone;
bribes, betrayals. I am lying
even now. Can you believe
that? I give you my word.

Coming Down Cleveland Avenue

The fumes from all kinds
of machines have dirtied
the snow. You propose
to polish it, the miles
between home and wherever
you and your lily
of a woman might go. You
go, pail, brush, and
suds, scrubbing down
Cleveland Avenue
toward the Hartford Life
Insurance Company. No
one appreciates your
effort and one important
character calls you
a baboon. But pretty
soon your darling jumps
out of an elevator
and kisses you and you
sing and tell her to
walk the white plains
proudly. At one point
you even lay down
your coat, and she, in
turn, puts hers down for
you. And you put your
shirt down, and she, her
blouse, and your pants,
and her skirt, shoes—
removes her lavender
underwear and you slip
into her proud, white skin.

Reapers of the Water

The nets newly tarred
and the family arranged
on deck—Mass has started.

The archbishop in
his golden
cope and tall miter, a resplendent

figure against an unwonted background, the darting
silver of water,
green and lavender

of the hyacinths, the slow
movement of occasional
boats. Incense floats

up and about the dripping gray
moss and the sound of the altar bell
rings out. Automatically all who have stayed

on their boats drop to their knees with the others
on shore. The prelate, next taking up his sermon,
recalls that the disciples of Christ were drawn

from the fishermen
of Galilee. Through
the night, at the lake, they cast in vain.

Then He told
them to try once more, and lo!
the nets came heavily loaded. . . . Now

there will be days when
you, too, will
cast your nets without success—be not

discouraged; His all-seeing
eye will be
on you. And in the storm, when

your boat tosses like a thin
leaf, hold firm. . . .
Who knows whose man will be next? Grandmère

whose face describes how three of hers—
her husband and those two boys—had not returned,
now looks toward

her last son—
it is a matter of time.
The prelate dips his gold aspergillum

into the container of holy water
and lifts it high. As the white
and green boats

pass, the drops fall on the scrubbed
decks, on the nets, on the shoulders
of the nearest ones, and they move up

the long waterway.
The crowds watching and waving:
the *Sea Dream*, the *Normandie*,

the *Barbara Coast*, the *Little Hot
Dog*, the *God
Bless America*, the *Madame of Q.*—

racing past the last tendrils
of the warm pudding
that is Louisiana.

Epithalamion for Tyler

I thought I knew something
about loneliness but
you go to the stockyards

buy a pig's ear and sew
it on your couch. That, you
said, is my best friend—we

have spirited talks. Even
then I thought: a man of
such exquisite emptiness

(and you cultivated it so)
is ground for fine flowers.

For Mother on Father's Day

You never got to recline
in the maternal tradition,
I never let you. Fate,

you call it, had other eyes,
for neither of us ever had
a counterpart in the way

familial traditions go.
I was your brother,
and you were my unhappy

neighbor. I pitied you
the way a mother pities
her son's failure. I could

never find the proper
approach. I would have
lent you sugar, mother.

In a Town for Which
I Know No Name

I think of your blind odor
too long till I collide with
barbers, and am suspected.

The clerk malingers when I
nod. I am still afraid of
the natural. Even the

decrepit animals,
coveting their papers and
curbs, awake and go breathing

through the warm darkness of
hotel halls. I think that they
are you coming back from the

colossal obscurity
of your exhausted passions,
and dash to the door again.

Success Comes to Cow Creek

I sit on the tracks,
a hundred feet from
earth, fifty from the
water. Gerald is
inching toward me
as grim, slow, and
determined as a
season, because he
has no trade and wants
none. It's been nine months
since I last listened
to his fate, but I
know what he will say:
he's the fire hydrant
of the underdog.

When he reaches my
point above the creek,
he sits down without
salutation, and
spits profoundly out
past the edge, and peeks
for meaning in the
ripple it brings. He
scowls. He speaks: when you
walk down any street
you see nothing but
coagulations
of shit and vomit,
and I'm sick of it.
I suggest suicide;
he prefers murder,
and spits again for
the sake of all the
great devout losers.

A conductor's horn
concerto breaks the
air, and we, two doomed
pennies on the track,
shove off and somersault
like anesthetized
fleas, ruffling the
ideal locomotive
poised on the water
with our light, dry bodies.
Gerald shouts
terrifically as
he sails downstream like
a young man with a
destination. I
swim toward shore as
fast as my boots will
allow; as always,
neglecting to drown.

Why I Will Not Get Out of Bed

My muscles unravel
like spools of ribbon:
there is not a shadow

of pain. I will pose
like this for the rest
of the afternoon,

for the remainder
of all noons. The rain
is making a valley

of my dim features.
I am in Albania,
I am on the Rhine.

It is autumn,
I smell the rain,
I see children running

through columbine.
I am honey,
I am several winds.

My nerves dissolve,
my limbs wither—
I don't love you.

I don't love you.

Graveside

Rodina Feldervatova,
the community's black angel—
well, we come to you,

having failed to sink
our own webbed fingers
in the chilled earth where

you hang out. I think
you are doomed to become
symbols for us that we

will never call by name.
But what rifles through
our heads is silence, one

either beyond or below
whatever it is that we do
know. We know by heart,

don't we? We've never
learned. And we bring what
we have known to you, now,

tonight. Open your home
to us, Rodina. Kiss
our brains. Tell us that

we are not drunk, and
that we may spend
our summers with you.

The Lost Pilot

for my father, 1922–1944

Your face did not rot
like the others—the co-pilot,
for example, I saw him

yesterday. His face is corn-
mush: his wife and daughter,
the poor ignorant people, stare

as if he will compose soon.
He was more wronged than Job.
But your face did not rot

like the others—it grew dark,
and hard like ebony;
the features progressed in their

distinction. If I could cajole
you to come back for an evening,
down from your compulsive

orbiting, I would touch you,
read your face as Dallas,
your hoodlum gunner, now,

with the blistered eyes, reads
his braille editions. I would
touch your face as a disinterested

scholar touches an original page.
However frightening, I would
discover you, and I would not

turn you in; I would not make
you face your wife, or Dallas,
or the co-pilot, Jim. You

could return to your crazy
orbiting, and I would not try
to fully understand what

it means to you. All I know
is this: when I see you,
as I have seen you at least

once every year of my life,
spin across the wilds of the sky
like a tiny, African god,

I feel dead. I feel as if I were
the residue of a stranger's life,
that I should pursue you.

My head cocked toward the sky,
I cannot get off the ground,
and, you, passing over again,

fast, perfect, and unwilling
to tell me that you are doing
well, or that it was mistake

that placed you in that world,
and me in this; or that misfortune
placed these worlds in us.

Intimidations of an Autobiography

I am walking a trail
on a friend's farm
about three miles from

town. I arrange the day
for you. I stop and say,
you would not believe how happy

I was as a child,
to some logs. Blustery wind
puts tumbleweed

in my face as I am
pretending to be on my way
home to see you and

the family again,
to touch the orange
fingers of the moon.

That's how I think of it.
The years flipped back last night
and I drank hot rum till

dawn.
It was a wild success and I wasn't sad when
I woke past noon

and saw the starlings in the sky.
My brain's an old rag anyway,
but I've got a woman and you'd say

she's too good for me. You'd call
her a real doll and me a goof-ball.
I've got my head between my paws

because it's having a damn
birthday party. How old do you think I am?
I bet you think I'm

seventeen.
It doesn't matter. Just between
us, you know what I'm doing

now? I'm calling the cows home.
They're coming, too.
I lower

myself to the ground lazily,
a shower of avuncular kisses
issuing from my hands and lips—

I just wanted to tell you
I remember you even now;
Goodbye, goodbye. Here come the cows.

The End of the Line

We plan in partial sleep
a day of intense activity—
to arrive at a final bargain

with the deaf grocer,
to somehow halt a train;
we plan our love's rejuvenation

one last time. And then
she dreams another life
altogether. I've gone away.

The petals of a red bud
caught in a wind between
Hannibal and Carthage,

the day has disappeared.
Like a little soap bubble
the moon glides around

our bed. We are two negroes
lugubriously sprawled
on a parched boardwalk.

The Move

. . . you are alone with the Alone,
and it is His move.
             Robert Penn Warren

The old buccaneers are leaving
now. They have had
their fill. A blue halo

has circled the imitation
gold, and the real, and they
are bewildered. All

is shimmering. The sea
is shimmering like a marvelous belly
viewed from the outside

during a blizzard in the mountains.
For each other
they are shimmering.

They do not know what splendor
is balanced
atop the foresail now, what

it is that is moving, moving
toward them, down.
They rub their bodies.

The skin is a fine lace
of salt and disease,
and something is moving

just under the skin
and they know
that it is not blood.

Flight

for K.

Like a glum cricket
the refrigerator is singing
and just as I am convinced

that it is the only noise
in the building, a pot falls
in 2B. The neighbors on

both sides of me suddenly
realize that they have not
made love to their wives

since 1947. The racket
multiplies. The man downhall
is teaching his dog to fly.

The fish are disgusted
and beat their heads blue
against a cold aquarium. I too

lose control and consider
the dust huddled in the corner
a threat to my endurance.

Were you here, we would not
tolerate mongrels in the air,
nor the conspiracies of dust.

We would drive all night,
your head tilted on my shoulder.
At dawn, I would nudge you

with my anxious fingers and say,
Already we are in Idaho.

Grace

The one thing that sustained
the faces on the four
corners of the intersection

did not unite them,
did not invite others to join.
Their inner eyes as the light

changed did not change,
but focused madly precise
on the one thing until

it scared them. Then
they all went to the movies.
I was just beginning

to understand when one
who represented the desperate
shrunken state came toward

me, bisecting the whole mass
of concrete into triangles;
and handed me a package.

I carried it with me for
the rest of my life, never
opening it, telling no one.

The Last Days of April

Through the ceiling comes
the rain to cool my lover
and me. The lime carpeting

darkens, and when we cross
to retrieve our glasses
of gin from the mantle, our

feet sink as into drifts
of leaves. We have a deep
thirst, for it is the end

of April, and we know that
a great heat is coming soon
to deaden these passions.

Uncle

Homer was a ventriloquist;
so drunk, one day he projected his voice
so far it just

kept going and going (still is).
Joe Ray insisted
Homer was afraid of work, but he's

had 130 jobs or more
just recently, he didn't think in terms
of careers.

The family never
cared for Homer
even after

he ginned himself into a wall
and died balling
with a deaf-mute in an empty Kansas City hall.

Joe Ray insisted
Homer would have made a fine dentist
had he kept his mouth shut; that is,

had he lived. Still is
heard about the house
jiggling glasses,

his devoted astral voice coming back.

How the Friends Met

So what do you do? What
can you do? Leave the room
altogether? Crazy.
Your eyes are the wallpaper;
makes it tough, doesn't it?
Peel them away. You call
that pain? It's not. It's insane.

You make it. Keep going.
Confront a lightpole. Smoke
a mythopoeic
cigarette forever.
Mark a spot with your
mysterious shoe; scratch
Hate in the sidewalk.

A man will come along
and there will be reason
enough to knife him. Sure
enough, there comes along
a worse-than-Bogart. . . .
There you are, smoking
the lightpole. The spot

you marked appears between
your eyes, and then becomes
a sidewalk, and the man
walks right up the sidewalk
into your room, looks at
the wallpaper, and laughs.
So what do you do? What

can you do? Kick him out?
Hell, no. You charge him rent.

Tragedy Comes to the Bad Lands

Amnesic goatherds tromboning
on the summit, the lazy
necklaces of their own breath
evanesce into the worst
blizzard since Theodore
Roosevelt and the Marquis
de Mores blessed Medora, North
Dakota with their rugged
presence. Look! I implore, who's
sashaying across the Bad
Lands now—it's trepid riding
Tate (gone loco in the
cabeza) out of his little
civilized element—Oh!
It's bound to end in tears.

Aunt Edna

Aunt Edna of the hills
comes down to give
her sisters chills;

she wears the same
rags she wore
seven years ago,

she smells
the same, she tells
the same hell-

is-here stories.
She hates flowers,
she hates the glory

of the church she
abandoned for the
glory

of her Ozark cave.
She gave
her sons to the wolves.

Rescue

For the first time the only
thing you are likely to break

is everything because
it is a dangerous

venture. Danger invites
rescue—I call it loving.

We've got a good thing
going—I call it rescue.

Nicest thing ever to come
between steel cobwebs, we hope

so. A few others should get
around to it, I can't understand

it. There is plenty of room,
clean windows, we start our best

engines, a-rumm . . . everything is
relevant. I call it loving.

The Mirror

She tells me
that I can
see right through
her, but I
look and can
see nothing:

so we go
ahead and
kiss. She is
fine glass, I
say, throwing
her to the
floor. . . .

The Tabernacle

Poor God was always there,
but He was something sinister,
and we worshiped the fear

we had of Him,
we had of the church on Tenth,
near the end

of the whole dark city.
The way the family
gathered murmuring on a Sunday,

surreptitious, solemn,
down to the midwest harlem
to give our worn

and rusty souls an airing—
grandmother swearing
at Ruthanna's hoop ear-rings,

and Uncle Barrington,
hesitant, knowing what would come,
stealing his Sunday swill of rum

invariably. Once there, it was not
as bad as we had thought;
it was not God at all, but

Pentecostal
joy. A man would wrestle
with his soul, and all

the other sinners cheered,
and soon we heard
the voices of another tongue—

garbled, and far too
inflated for us
to understand who

taught them how to sing such songs.

Late Harvest

I look up and see
a white buffalo
emerging from the
enormous red gates
of a cattle truck
lumbering into
the mouth of the sun.
The prairie chickens
do not seem to fear
me; neither do the
girls in cellophane
fields, near me, hear me
changing the flat tire
on my black tractor.
I consider screaming
to them; then, night comes.

Today I Am Falling

A sodium pentothal landscape,
a bud about to break open—
I want to be there, ambassador
to the visiting blossoms, first
to breathe their smothered, secret
odors. Today I am falling, falling,
falling in love, and desire
to leave this place forever.

II

from The Oblivion Ha-Ha

(1 9 7 0)

Poem

High in Hollywood Hills a door opens:
a man disguised as a man appears,

sunglasses on his nose, a beard.
He can smell the flowers—camellia,
bougainvillea—the word,

itself a dream; the reality of the scene
was in the Chinese girl

who swam in the pool beneath
the rail he leaned on:
she was something else indeed.

She was the dream within
the dream within. He shouted: hallo,

halloo.
He did the handkerchief dance all alone.
O Desire! it is the beautiful dress

for which the proper occasion
never arises.

O the wedding cake and the good cigar!
O the souvenir ashtray!

Rape in the Engineering Building

What I saw on his face scared me—ants
on jelly; two cars ducked as he zigzagged

past the library up to the tracks
where the other students were just falling

from classes. One big man yelled,
stop him stop that man, but I thought

it was personal and got out of their
way. Finally the aproned man told us

in a high stuck voice it was rape
in the engineering building, and

the rapist was chugging farther up
the inclined edge of town into

the shadowy upright garden.
Full of thanks, we took after him.

The Blue Booby

The blue booby lives
on the bare rocks
of Galápagos
and fears nothing.
It is a simple life:
they live on fish,
and there are few predators.
Also, the males do not
make fools of themselves
chasing after the young
ladies. Rather,
they gather the blue
objects of the world
and construct from them

a nest—an occasional
Gaulois package,
a string of beads,
a piece of cloth from
a sailor's suit. This
replaces the need for
dazzling plumage;
in fact, in the past
fifty million years
the male has grown
considerably duller,
nor can he sing well.
The female, though,

asks little of him—
the blue satisfies her
completely, has
a magical effect
on her. When she returns

from her day of
gossip and shopping,
she sees he has found her
a new shred of blue foil:
for this she rewards him
with her dark body,
the stars turn slowly
in the blue foil beside them
like the eyes of a mild savior.

The Pet Deer

The Indian Princess
   in her apricot tea gown
moves through the courtyard
   teasing the pet deer

as if it were her lover.
   The deer, so small and
confused, slides on the marble
   as it rises on its hind legs

towards her, slowly, and with
   a sad, new understanding.
She does not know what
   the deer dreams or desires.

Up Here

The motel was made for love
as you were. I undressed you
with grace and tenderness,
kissing each newly bared part.

There you lay, your small, white
body throbbing in my hand
like a bird. We were silent.
The right word was not needed.

Supple. What was I doing
suddenly pacing around
the bed, scratching my head,
staring down at your gaze up
at me? *Recognition.*

I would not call you *svelte.*
Your breasts were barely a hand-
ful; I like small breasts, which fit
a hand. Your thighs were a feast,
though, and, walking, now and then
I would dip down to nibble
them. They were good: *wholesome.*
They were the bread of life.

Now your lips are moving, now
your hands reach up at me.
I feel as if I might be one
or two thousand feet above you.
Your lips form something, a bubble,
which rises and rises into
my hand: inside it is a word:
Help. I would like to help,
believe me, but up here nothing
is possible, nothing is clear:
Help. Help me.

Prose Poem

I am surrounded by the pieces of this huge
puzzle: here's a piece I call my wife, and
here's an odd one I call convictions, here's
conventions, here's collisions, conflagrations,
congratulations. Such a puzzle this is! I
like to grease up all the pieces and pile
them in the center of the basement after
everyone else is asleep. Then I leap head-
first like a diver into the wretched confusion.
I kick like hell and strangle a few pieces,
bite them, spitting and snarling like a mongoose.
When I wake up in the morning, it's all fixed!
My wife says she would not be caught dead at
that savage resurrection. I say she would.

Coda

Love is not worth so much;
I regret everything.
Now on our backs
in Fayetteville, Arkansas,
the stars are falling
into our cracked eyes.

With my good arm
I reach for the sky,
and let the air out of the moon.
It goes whizzing off
to shrivel and sink
in the ocean.

You cannot weep;
I cannot do anything
that once held an ounce
of meaning for us.
I cover you
with pine needles.

When morning comes,
I will build a cathedral
around our bodies.
And the crickets,
who sing with their knees,
will come there
in the night to be sad,
when they can sing no more.

The Tryst

In the early evening rain
I leave the vault
and walk into the city

of lamentations, and stand.
I think it is September, September.

Where are you, Josephine?
It is one minute until you must appear,
draped in a grass-green serape,

shorter than most people,
more beautiful, baleful . . .

pressing a hand to my forehead,
slipping into my famished pocket
the elixir, the silver needle.

Pity Ascending with the Fog

He had no past and he certainly
had no future. All the important
events were ending shortly before
they began. He says he told mama

earth what he would not accept: and I
keep thinking it had something to do
with her world. Nights expanding into
enormous parachutes of fire, his

eyes were little more than mercury.
Or sky-diving in the rain when there
was obviously no land beneath,
half-dead fish surfacing all over

his body. He knew all this too well.
And she who might at any time be
saying the word that would embrace all
he had let go, he let go of course.

I think the pain for him will end in
May or January, though the weather
is far too clear for me to think of
anything but august comedy.

Pride's Crossing

Where the railroad meets the sea,
I recognize her hand.
Where the railroad meets the sea,
her hair is as intricate as a thumbprint.
Where the railroad meets the sea,
her name is the threshold of sleep.

Where the railroad meets the sea,
it takes all night to get there.
Where the railroad meets the sea,
you have stepped over the barrier.
Where the railroad meets the sea,
you will understand afterwards.

Where the railroad meets the sea,
where the railroad meets the sea—
I know only that our paths lie together,
and you cannot endure if you remain alone.

The Indian Undertaker

There is a man carrying an armload of lilacs
across the field: he may be a lost Indian
as he is whistling, very beautifully, a tune
to the birds I have never heard. I am in back
of him, following at a distance. Three small quail,
perhaps hypnotized, rise and circle his head.
I want to stop the man and ask him what he said
to make them feel so safe, but I feel
weak and dizzy. His whistling begins to chill
my neck, as if the wind from his lips were
rushing round me. If only I were agile
like this family of field mice heading for
the river; still, I am not sorry I came here.

A lilac is falling like a piece of sky
from his arms; it seems to take ten minutes or more.
Finally it kisses the wet earth. I
start running—the lilac is waiting for me.
Here you are! I feel the first emotions of love.
And, look, a snail is holding on to your leaf
for all he's worth. So slowly he moves,
humming a psalm to the god of snails.
The lilac swoons. The ground is sapphire
and the trees are topaz. I feel as if I were
attending my own funeral, the air a jail
of music and cool yellow fire.

The Initiation

The long wake continues,
quiet and moronic expressions.
The jowl of the dead
is agape with infinite abandon
as if he were about to sing:
if we concentrate
he may remember the words.

In comes a man with a dog
on a chain; then several others.
The room is bathed
in plaster of paris.
In the background
a deep, abundant fugue has begun.
The piece is dedicated
to me. How strange,
I thought I was new here.

They stop playing,
file quickly into another room.
As I begin to leave
shafts of darkness reach out
and close the little door.

Consumed

Why should you believe in magic,
pretend an interest in astrology
or the tarot? Truth is, you are

free, and what might happen to you
today, nobody knows. And your
personality may undergo a radical

transformation in the next half
hour. So it goes. You are consumed
by your faith in justice, your

hope for a better day, the rightness
of fate, the dreams, the lies
the taunts—Nobody gets what he

wants. A dark star passes through
you on your way home from
the grocery: never again are you

the same—an experience which is
impossible to forget, impossible
to share. The longing to be pure

is over. You are the stranger
who gets stranger by the hour.

Shadowboxing

Sometimes you almost get a punch in.
Then you may go for days without even seeing him,
or his presence may become a comfort
for a while.

He says: I saw you scrambling last night
on your knees and hands.

He says: How come you always want to be
something else, how come you never take your life
seriously?

And you say: Shut up! Isn't it enough
I say I love you, I give you everything!

He moves across the room with his hand
on his chin, and says: How great you are!

Come here, let me touch you, you say.

He comes closer. Come close, you say.
He comes closer. Then. *Whack!* And
you start again, moving around and around
the room, the room which grows larger
and larger, darker and darker. The black moon.

Images of Little Compton, Rhode Island

Here the tendons in the swans' wings stretch,
feel the tautness of their futuristic necks,
imagine their brains' keyhole accuracy,
envy their infinitely precise desires.

A red-nosed Goodyear zeppelin emerges from the mist
like an ethereal albino whale on drugs.

One wanders around a credible hushed town.

Mosquito hammering through the air
with a horse's power: there will be no cameramen.
We will swap bodies maybe
giving the old one a shove.

That's an awful lot of work for you I said
and besides look at your hands,
there are small fires in the palms,
there is smoke squirting from every pore.

O when all is lost,
when we have thrown our shoes in the sea,
when our watches have crawled off into weeds,
our typewriters have finally spelled perhaps
accidentally the unthinkable word,

when the rocks loosen and the sea anemones
welcome us home with their gossamer arms
dropping like a ship from the stars,

what on earth shall we speak or think of,
and who do you think you are?

From the Hole

A horse-drawn rocket
climbs the wooden hill:
behind it two or three friends
are sharing their tobacco: their hats
are beautiful like small pieces of
coal on their heads
fostering goodwill.
I'm standing in this hole, see,
and I'm going to holler out:
"Good riddance to bad rubbish!"
and "I'm sorry if I was a menace!"
"Howdy doody, milkman travail!"
"So long buoys and grills."
Like a harp
burning on an island
nobody knows about.

The Trap

Inside the old chair
I found another chair;
though smaller, I liked
sitting in it better.
Inside that chair
I found another chair;
though smaller, in
many ways I felt
good sitting in it.
Inside that chair
I found another chair;
it was smaller and
seemed to be made
just for me.
Inside that chair,
still another;
it was very small,
so small I could
hardly get out of it.
Inside that chair
I found yet another;
and in that, another,
and another, until
I was sitting in
a chair so small
it would be difficult
to say I was sitting
in a chair at all.
I could not rise
or fall, and no one
could catch me.

Twilight Sustenance Hiatus

The relentless confetti of dollars!
I'd prefer to kiss that silent chipmunk
on the roadside while a tiny ocean
of dandelion seeds arranges a gray
throne on his ear! I have no "final"
vows to take tonight, though your hair
might be floating down the Ohio.
Chameleons can march around a small room
if they want. I could sell gasoline

on the desert, though I would miss
the grass. Or I could even get your name
tattooed gingerly across my wrist at dawn.
There is so little news fit to print:
yesterday a moth caught fire.
Today a lost school of astronomers
came back. We only think tomorrow
is called "The Finished Gem."
Tomorrow is called . . . come on.

The Wheelchair Butterfly

O sleepy city of reeling wheelchairs
where a mouse can commit suicide if he can

concentrate long enough
on the history book of rodents
in this underground town

of electrical wheelchairs!
The girl who is always pregnant and bruised
like a pear

rides her many-stickered bicycle
backward up the staircase
of the abandoned trolleybarn.

Yesterday was warm. Today a butterfly froze
in midair; and was plucked like a grape
by a child who swore he could take care

of it. O confident city where
the seeds of poppies pass for carfare,

where the ordinary hornets in a human's heart
may slumber and snore, where bifocals bulge

in an orange garage of daydreams,
we wait in our loose attics for a new season

as if for an ice-cream truck.
An Indian pony crosses the plains

whispering Sanskrit prayers to a crater of fleas.
Honeysuckle says: I thought I could swim.

The Mayor is urinating on the wrong side
of the street! A dandelion sends off sparks:
beware your hair is locked!

Beware the trumpet wants a glass of water!
Beware a velvet tabernacle!

Beware the Warden of Light has married
an old piece of string!

It's Not the Heat So Much as the Humidity

Only a dish of blueberries could pull me
out of this lingering funk.
I'm tired of taking the kids down
to watch the riot, no longer impressed
with fancy electrical nets, sick
of supersonic nightsticks.

Buy myself a hot dog and a glass of beer—
that helps. It's hard to say
who's winning. Nobody is winning.

Boy, Kansas City! Big Zoo! Oriental art!
Starlight Theater: *Annie Get Your Gun*
going into its seventeenth year.
Once I met Tab Hunter there, four o'clock
in the morning, standing in line

at the Coke machine, so tall and blond,
though not much of a conversationalist.

It's good to be home, trying to soften
the blow for young girls who are inclined
to fall off their porches.

Some of my best friends are . . .
Curse on those who do or do not take dope.

When Autumn comes, O when Fall arrives,
in her chemise of zillion colors,
I will sigh noisily, as if an old and
disgusting leg had finally dropped off.

No more drinking beer, no more
the perpetual search for an air-
conditioned friend, no more friends.

I'll take piano lessons, French lessons,
speed-reading lessons, and if there is
still time to kill, gawk at a bluejay
tumbling out of the maple tree.

Cars slide by with their windows up,
whispering of a Mexican Restaurant
"with really good Chili Verde."

The gutters billow with mauve death;
a mother's sad voice sends out
a tugboat whistle through the purple mist:
she worries about her children.

And the dangerous fishhook of melancholy
dangles from every dog's ear.
The dog that saved my life,
that keeps on saving it each long, humid night.
The dead dog. And so:

a shiny baseball hovers over the city.
No one asks why. And so: it passes on.
And so: a telephone starts to ring
in a widow's cake-filled kitchen . . .

A rollerskate collides with a lunchpail.

The Eagle Exterminating Company

There are birds larger than us, I know that.
There is a bird in the bedroom much larger than the bed.
There is a photograph of a dead bird somewhere,
    I can't remember.
There is a wingspan that would put us all in the shadows.

There is the birdcall I must anticipate each night.
There are feathers everywhere.
Everywhere you walk there are feathers, you can try
to hop over and between them but then
you look like a bird. You are too small to be one.

You look like a tiny one-winged bird.
If you are your mother will come and kill you.
If you are not you will probably beat yourself to death.

But what matters is that every room in the house is filled,
is filled with the cry of the eagle.
Exterminating the eagles is now all but impossible
for the house would fall down without them.

There is a photograph of a dead bird somewhere.
Everywhere you walk there are feathers.
You look like a tiny one-winged bird.
There is the birdcall. There is the wingspan.

The President Slumming

In a weird, forlorn voice
he cries: it is a mirage!
Then tosses a wreath of scorpions
to the children,
mounts his white nag
and creeps off into darkness,
smoking an orange.

Failed Tribute to the Stonemason of Tor House, Robinson Jeffers

We traveled down to see your house,
Tor House, Hawk Tower, in Carmel,
California. It was not quite what
I thought it would be: I wanted it
to be on a hill, with a view of the ocean
unobstructed by other dwellings.
Fifty years ago I know you had
a clean walk to the sea, hopping
from boulder to boulder, the various
seafowl rightly impressed with
your lean, stern face. But today

with our cameras cocked we had to
sneak and crawl through trimmed lawns
to even verify the identity of
your strange carbuncular creation,
now rented to trillionaire non-
literary folk from Pasadena.
Edged in on all sides by trilevel
pasteboard phantasms, it took
a pair of good glasses to barely see
some newlyweds feed popcorn
to an albatross. Man *is*

a puny thing, divorced,
whether he knows it or not, and
pays his monthly alimony,
his child-support. Year after year
you strolled down to this exceptionally
violent shore and chose your boulder;
the arms grew as the house grew
as the mind grew to exist outside
of time, beyond the dalliance
of your fellows. Today I hate
Carmel: I seek libation in the Tiki

Bar: naked native ladies are painted
in iridescent orange on velvet cloth:
the whole town loves art.
And I donate this Singapore Sling
to the memory of it, and join
the stream of idlers simmering outside.
Much as hawks circled your head
when you cut stone all afternoon,
kids with funny hats on motorscooters
keep circling the block.
Jeffers, . . .

Conjuring Roethke

Prickle a lamb,
giggle a yam,
beat a chrysanthemum
out of its head
with a red feather.
Dream of a pencil
or three airmail stamps
under your pillow.
Thank the good fairy
you're not dead.

The heat's on,
the window's gone,
the ceiling is sorry
it hurt you.
But this is not air
holding your hand,
nor weasels beneath
your dirt rug.
I think the corks
are out of breath,
the bottles begin
laughing a zoo.

I wish you were here.
The calendar is red,
a candle closes
the room.
If this is the life
we are all leaving
it's half as bad.
Hello again mad turnip.
Let's tango together
down to the clear
glad river.

Dear Reader

I am trying to pry open your casket
with this burning snowflake.

I'll give up my sleep for you.
This freezing sleet keeps coming down
and I can barely see.

If this trick works we can rub our hands
together, maybe

start a little fire
with our identification papers.
I don't know but I keep working, working

half hating you,
half eaten by the moon.

III

from Hints to Pilgrims

(1 9 7 1)

Recipe for Sleep

knit the mosquitoes together
beneath your pajamas
let a stranger suck on your foot
reach inside of yourself
and pull out a candle
clutch the giant shrimp tighter

run down the staircase
inside a violet
eat through both doors
empty the hammock of its blood
uncork the head of a doll
and choke the rose inside of it

when you get to the glacial lake
wrap yourself up in gauze
and then swallow your hands

the reverse sometimes works
for waking

Brother of the Unknown Ancient Man

I think you are in love with more
than a story this is the story of
stories and what you have done with it

The food has been cooked the wine
has been chilled and the guest of
honor is at the bottom of the lake

He had a hunger for the flying
machine funny these white clouds
don't feel like toilet paper

Bony fingers of death heaven knows
when I'll be able to talk to anyone
like I'm talking to you now

I'm in a family way ninety-proof
fiction the party is next door
and that's the way it's always been

What manner of me are these
I hate airports too many airplanes
what could I ever do but love her

Brother of the unknown ancient man
he forsook all earthbound vanities
throw the dirt gently onto his grave.

When the Nomads Come
Over the Hill

When the nomads come over the hill
on the wheatstraw camels
the angel of joy crawls down a long hallway
and the green vegetables in the abandoned cart
pour into blue flames
old men by the fountain rise
and bid one another adieu
the bright sun is rinsed in blackest ink
snakes sleep on their backs
around the golden sundial
giant night hides in the storyteller's pupils
and the wind is divided
by a well-placed needle
when the nomads come over the hill
with their invisible language.

Poem

A silence that tunnels forever
through your eyes no no you have
no eyes an eyelash caught in the
doorjamb see I am crying I know
you are in there inside one of
these tears your body the color
of drunk water water thrown out
of a rocketship that's the only
water that quenches this thirst
your cricketblue body sizzling
like a sky of cinders a galaxy
born of laughter the cliff of
scent your own body is making
with each sigh you must guide
me elsewhere through the rain
a small man from another world
I am the canary that strangles
itself with joy and you my widow
floating through this mirror.

I Take Back All My Kisses

They got me because if a forest has no end I'll go naked
They got me because my mother stood at the edge of a runway
    for seven years with her head in her hands
They got me because an empty street is going on without us
They got me because when I drink wine I drink an ocean and
    when I drink from a river I drink a stranger's childhood
They got me because I suffered from whiplash in a dream
They got me because I got myself first and last
They got me inbetween
They came and got me at dawn in Missouri
They got me with hands like blond spatulas
I let them take me away because the sun was nearer than I
    expected and because I expected them to take me away
    and because I had never been there
They got me because I was elected to go by the dead
They got me because the dead have too many votes but such
    poor memories
They got me because the neighbors have wings
They got me because deer are hopeless in more ways than one
Because lights are turning on and off in my knees and I can be
    spotted through a yard of brick
They got me yesterday because I wore a see-through skullcap
    in the gymnasium of sudden deaths
Because I spit in the eye of the corner guillotine
Thunder Guggenheim got me today the fourth horseman
They got me today because a subway wrecked on your lifeline
They got me in kindergarten when I dropped the atomic bomb
J. Edgar Hoover got me for inventing the milkpod
The Preacher got me for eloping with a snail
I am convinced I am dizzy and should not be allowed to walk
    the streets of the city after dark alone
I am a menace to the diamonds that shiver in flowerbeds
They got me because I begged them to not take me more
    seriously than they take themselves
Because they believed me when I said I could not change them
Because they moved the curtains back expecting to see eternity

Because eternity was in back of them and I stood in front
As I promised I would never do though I lied
I lied because my feet were nailed to a ship of birds
They got me because a wall is nothing to another wall
Because I drove my heart into the ground with joy
As I promised I would never sigh as a tree in the garden of
    pleases
No ghost spoke to me of the blood that drew near me but was
    not mine
They got me because a chimney was found to remember
They got me suddenly I had been waiting too long
They got me Thursday it was not raining ragas and riches
They got me Monday I can recall the tiny noise
Saturday they got me my mouth was already gagged
They got me Wednesday a most forgettable day
They got me Tuesday, Sunday, they got me Friday
    how easy to unpack those yellowing odd days
Because fire is carried in a hat across the desert of birth
They got me because my job was to pluck houses from the
    blind
Because women were waiting at the needle of bookstores
Because windows are jumping in you and out of you
They got me with rubber horns and drugged rabbits
They got me when a rug was too tired to fly
They got me because I'm trembling beneath a stove
They got me because I stalk the stone in daylight
They got me because caresses are molded into poems
Yes I never said I didn't fall into their hands like mercury
Mercury eaten in a fish
Mercury flashed across an afternoon nightmare
Tomorrow may be different
Who will be the last to know

Frivolous Blind Death Child

The lake was filled with wax,
and the ducks were wax.
The reeds were wax reeds,
and the wind was a waxy wind.

How beautiful you are
asleep in my arms.
So as not to waken you
I gladly cut them off.

Frivolous blind death child
covered with stardust,
why do you stick your tongue
inside the clock,
why do you follow me
into the toolshed?

You have a third mouth
where most people hide
their third eye.

Can you taste the gold mountain,
can you taste the gold flower,
can you taste the gold knife?
No, no! That is the gold butterfly!

Alternatives

I

Don't you see?
I have nothing left;
I have no home.
I don't mean that,
not always,
not only,
no more.

Don't mention it.

II

If, whether, suppose.
If you like.
If you only knew!
If nothing else,
if anything,
even if.

Otherwise, if not.
At least.

III

He was beside himself.
He did it by himself.
He shifted for himself.
He's talking to himself.
He put it in his pocket.
He's laughing at it.
He went off.

IV

Between, among, amongst.
Between ourselves, amongst friends.
To myself.
All things considered.

V

Things, goods, wares, clothes.
What a lot of stuff!
To speak badly of someone.
Food, victuals.
That's a fine state of affairs!
That's a fine thing, indeed!

A heap of stuff!
It isn't your stuff,
other people's property.
Rubbish, trash.

VI

Demure person,
to look as though butter
would melt in one's mouth.
To have a slight love affair,
to fall in love a little,
to retire into the shell,
to grow fat,
to grow stiff,
jamming one's hat over one's eyes,
to swallow.

VII

To stop, to plug, to cork,
to bung, to stuff up.
To stop someone's mouth.
To stop up a hole.
To stop a tooth.

To be stopped,
to become obstructed.
To stop one's ears,
to hold one's nose.

Your family, my people.
To thunder, to roar.

VIII

To settle on and work a farm.
To train vines on poplars.
To give something not wanted
or of little value.

To clap one's hands.
To hang oneself
at the foot of the bed.
At the foot of the page
to hang on.

IX

To have one's labor in vain.
To pay a debt.
Airpocket.
Burnt matter.
To burn oneself,
continual shivering.
To swam with people,
Courage!
Proof against anything,
bomb-proof.

X

The corner of a handkerchief,
cirriform of clouds.
Hither, on this side,
to speak in a low voice,
a barmaid, a stutterer,
to stagger, continuous staggering.
I regret very much to inform you.
To treat gently.
To shrivel unsown.

Amnesia People

Have we not gathered here because
a machine with thousands of tiny gears
sucking the air out of the room
considering Amanda's feverish condition
the gun fired and the picture-tube exploded
I found myself polishing my old wing-
tipped shoes his laconic master
had gone loco and I'll tell you why.

What did I have to gain I never
wanted anything but privacy just
as I was pulling on my suspenders
at which point I donned my hat
one could become always a zombie
he watched her bouncy walk
all his former existences wings for you
it was so natural now only happy thoughts.

Sometimes a man a stranger should be
allowed to put his hand on your shoulder
it had a life of its own
there was no evidence of life
he always knew it was terribly important
he did not know what else it could be
what is red and what is not red
it will be memorable a general blue.

The eyes of a deer a strange beauty indeed
her nose was dripping blood
a pattern of small rosebuds across her chest
which was itself small recurrent amnesia
he would give her a different story each time
the very quietest ones and in fact did
with nothing to go by until she finally
collapsed about the wonderful things.

If I were to attempt to trace
a barroom discussion of aesthetics
had devoured the symbolists
that certainly perked me up a bit
meant less than nothing to me
a pathological liar no more
than dimestore reproductions
red and black with fatigue.

Running further and further into
the countryside if we drank at all
according to the label
we had to pour it in our hair
no talking for two weeks
during electric storms at night
of course we could have just walked
into the graveyard and dug the damned thing up.

We settled on a little pebble
a couple of large steak dinners
thanks to the ignorance of some
local minister because he knew
his son was a genius with
the engine revved a last goodbye
for he could not be called a man
the car could be too easily traced.

I got postcards from Mexico
for which I loved him so
a good eastern asylum his life
long dream sliced open the world
and was allowed to fly
these dots were in fact human
falling off at an incredible rate
wham! wham! like that.

III

Conversations must be kept very low
will I understand them
I will be transformed into a lover
which they will riddle with bullets

no distinguishing marks at all
as it should be how I envied those
sighs that picture will come in handy
an electrifying performance.

I have been to this mansion many times
I have a chauffeur I do not recall
having ever tasted champagne
there is smoke everywhere
with the same weak spirit
studying the housewives with profound
distrust she detests cereal
the deal must have gone through.

Underwear everywhere see you next week
don't wake the dead did I have a hobby
a long time coming realization
from the stuff of life
people have travelled considerable distances
most would turn back it must be said
each doll can ask one question
for hours he will stare into the night.

I don't need this one anymore
with growing unrest and disgust
the deepest voice in the world
he laughed less and less
he could not even feel them
morning will tell no secrets
the fountain has been turned off
see her disappear too.

IV

No one in his right mind would come here
slowly rise and extend his arm
each one of us as he goes home tonight
and for the following week must search
his mind for lovely shorelines and
majestic mountains which took place in
the back of the hardware store having
obligations elsewhere on the sofa.

Who tried so hard to be good being the
veteran of fifty such scenes and his
family suffered greatly from it
would not let him sleep in the morning
they had an investment in lifetime
cafes can't last much longer over the years
a neighbor was easily dispensed with
for lack of better ground.

The next day a number of similar ideas
some had yardsticks for the first time
in seventy years for God knows somebody
had even taken landscape gardening
where she slept with her head on the table
such an enthusiastic response these
dead souls still contain smiling behind
the counter now it was bright yellow.

Very few people remembered or at least
bothered to recall his name rumor of
the transformation though still struggling
to keep his balance on the ladder
who had been drunk so long and taken
their lunch hours to drive over and observe
to find out what was really behind
a few pleasures which he could not find.

v

Still considered a disaster area
the mines went dry forty years ago
the town is as bright as it is
there are the fairs to anticipate
but the hours and days and years
are spent the endless games they
pretend to fight but it is all part
of the game innumerable excuses.

They need a nail on which to hang
they need a washer some seed they
need an opinion which is what the
customer wanted anyway from there
he fled the terrors he did not return

to his ship after three years of
loneliness with many things on his
mind though he was not senile.

As one who has observed the passing
of many debacles the soil of the earth
moves slowly and precisely dusting
through the shelves touching and
arranging them in comes Carl and
needs a spray for his tomatoes he
can sleep on Amabulae's porch until
he has redeemed himself two dollars.

The women are beautiful and unclean
make remarkable gadgets and toys
they swim all spring and summer
come out only to badger September
knowing how to detect the bite
how to fill their stomachs' reflection
anxious faces peering into it
the seasons are finally the greatest events
at least one reason to celebrate.

VI

In the simplest language he had nailed
it down and it glared at us
the unforgivable truth very much
wanted to be alone the whole
disgusting melodrama suddenly flying off
like a rosegarden not even depressed
about having his leg removed
give the guy a sucker.

Almost inaudible though piercing
head over heels through space
not hitting the earth forever
through the black carpet
ran my tongue over the pages
what do I do for a living
I have found myself a title monkeywrench
my own laughter quaked me.

Someone is always referring to his papers
I do not say machine pejoratively
so what keeps us together
I am continually surprised how few
find it in the least bit enticing
but for those who are motivated by courtesy
I reward with the truth
as if we were making a small attempt at hockey.

You are an unfortunate audience
I can't tell you who but I sense it
keeping the tree at bay on his way out
you had seven heads I wish I could
live that long not the hatchet
then silence knocking over a vase
it seeps into my head the lucky dog
hoping to find the right one.

VII

Now things were coming back and
they were in small world he may have
been once but never again one could
bathe and by the second day the more
perceptive villager along a gravel road
before he dozed off to prove that he
was overcome ask him as a question
almost as though he were afraid.

When he spoke the silence I believe
you said this is my first visit
and was glad about it and then left
the ferry wharf when they were finally
separated that was over his suitcase
had bad luck and saw no sense in fiddling
back there as to imply that only an
idiot would not know its doorway.

His cigarette wasn't even lit
he would take the place for the night
but this called for the tea cup
inside of which a jukebox just as he

had sighed when leaving the bus
to avoid small talk and ordered
the fluttering of his wings
he didn't feel he didn't think.

That was important when a froggy voice
and didn't bother to check a dream
whatever else might happen
but he could not hear him that was
his punishment and look where I
ended up feigning an intense interest
in the god-awful tale to pay my
tribute because this is where it ended.

VIII

In order to find an empty compartment
for himself he had to sit on his hands
any kind of human being at all oh my
I fell in your lap and stood there
looking through the glass until you have
a first name like a toy in a bottle
he would have to kill him if not everywhere
if there is really a sign read it.

People like that were padlocked inside
a long hallway I was shaking as a reader
for instance and ordered a highball
to keep your mouth shut
one thing before you go to sleep
I went back out there and tried to talk
there is no sign he gripped the edge
gazing out into the icy wilderness.

It's something I don't normally talk about
he liked the way it sounded months
in advance I don't care how yet if I
hear another peep out of you a vision
of the old man following him everywhere
certainly not too hurriedly
where is it that you are nobody
his father and his father's substitute.

Who knows what I might do there
get a house or something he'll never
pull himself out of it probably born
in it that kind of thing was exactly
why he chose it something pure had fallen
off and then in broken jumps winning
him back to the bottle they are all
together now wake up the dumb.

IX

The two men looked utterly dismayed
and sure enough the street was buzzing
in empty orange crates emerged from
their houses with unctions for no
living man seemed bothered that of all
the people naturally terrified by the
size so he stayed twenty-one years
never really adjusting to the new radio.

The enticing title at some point this
thrilled him nearly starving himself
wild saloons with alas so many factories
cowboy traffic now he knew it was the
same dismal hat there was hope the money
the same evening departed from sleep
you want to work in the mines and
walking absolutely no direction.

An infection had settled in the mangled
bone assisting in the corn harvest
dreaming of the new clean faces with
sailing footballs the few disbelievers
who drifted in a cup of coffee
carried away by innermost thoughts
the apparent failure of the scheme
was looking like its old self again.

Hulking mass finally in vain he meant
to brighten the dull customers but
the town sure as hell in anybody's memory
and I don't like admitting a nice character

seldom drank after saying this
his thin lips revealed only too much
and decided to spend the first week
of their honeymoon in less than a minute.

x

He knew he was being watched
twenty-six years of hard labor
slumbering in the library
fraught with tentativeness
it was not a very convincing gesture
who had known about the appointment
if his antennae told him
that Darlene was somehow off the job.

Retrace his footsteps into the forest
I did it last time
I don't suppose you know about that
then you don't have to know anything
you think we're against you
and that somehow puts you in front
he cut himself yesterday
where he cut himself.

You spent the whole day at the lake praying
I'm the Daily Press how much blood
complete but easy to digest
we can play our little games too
perhaps you'd care for some spirits
some spirits we love you
for your predictability
you know from experience.

Without the language to make your plea
would I say a thing like that
that's the only thing I can think of
which brings us back to the reason
of your visit to his cold and lonely cottage
for our work we will need to be
ever so clear are you a bird
no one is going to touch you.

Fuck the Astronauts

I

Eventually we must combine nightmares
an angel smoking a cigarette on the steps
of the last national bank, said to me.
I put her out with my thumb. I don't need that
cheap talk I've got my own problems.
It was sad, exciting, and horrible.
It was exciting, horrible, and sad.
It was horrible, sad, and exciting.
It was inviting, mad, and deplorable.
It was adorable, glad, and enticing.
Eventually we must smoke a thumb
cheap talk I've got my own angel
on the steps of the problems the bank
said to me I don't need that.
I will take this one window
with its sooty maps and scratches
so that my dreams will remember
one another and so that my eyes will not
become blinded by the new world.

II

The flames don't dance or slither.
They have painted the room green.
Beautiful and naked, the wives
are sleeping before the fire.
Now it is out. The men have
returned to the shacks,
slayed creatures from the forest
floor across their white
stationwagons. That just about
does it, says the other,
dumping her bucket
over her head. Well, I guess

we got everything, says one,
feeling around in the mud,
as if for a child.
Now they remember they want
that mud, who can't remember
what they got up for.
They parcel it out: when
they are drunk enough
they go into town with
a bucket of mud, saying
we can slice it up into
windmills like a bloated cow.
Later, they paint the insides
of the shack black,
and sit sucking eggs all night,
they want something real, useful,
but there isn't anything.

III

I will engineer the sunrise
they have disassembled our shadows
our echoes are erased from the walls
your nipples are the skeletons of olives
your nipples are an oriental delight
your nipples blow away like cigarette papers
your nipples are the mouths of mutes
so I am not here any longer
skein of lightning
memory's dark ink in your last smile
where the stars have swallowed their train schedule
where the stars have drowned in their dark petticoats
like a sock of hamburger
receiving the lightning
into his clitoris
red on red the prisoner
confesses his waltz
through the corkscrew lightning
nevermind the lightning
in your teeth let's waltz
I am the hashish pinball machine
that rapes a piano.

Lewis and Clark Overheard in Conversation

then we'll get us some wine and spare ribs
then we'll get us some wine and spare ribs
then we'll get us some wine and spare ribs
then we'll get us some wine and spare ribs
then we'll get us some wine and spare ribs
then we'll get us some wine and spare ribs
then we'll get us some wine and spare ribs
then we'll get us some wine and spare ribs
then we'll get us some wine and spare ribs
then we'll get us some wine and spare ribs
then we'll get us some wine and spare ribs
then we'll get us some wine and spare ribs
then we'll get us some wine and spare ribs
then we'll get us some wine and spare ribs
then we'll get us some wine and spare ribs
then we'll get us some wine and spare ribs
then we'll get us some wine and spare ribs
then we'll get us some wine and spare ribs
then we'll get us some wine and spare ribs
then we'll get us some wine and spare ribs
then we'll get us some wine and spare ribs
then we'll get us some wine and spare ribs
then we'll get us some wine and spare ribs

IV

from Absences

(1 9 7 2)

Contagion

When I drink
I am the only man
in New York City.
There are no lights,
but I am used to that.
There are the staircases
that go forever upward
like the twisted branches

of a cemetery willow.
No one has climbed them
since prohibition.
And the overturned automobiles
stripped to their skeletons,
chewed clean
by the darkness.

Then I see the ember of
a cigarette in an alley,
and know that I am no longer
alone. One of us
is still shaking.
And has led the other
into some huddle of extinction.

Breathing

I heard something coming,
something like a motorcycle,
something horrible with pistons awry,
with camshafts about to fill the air
with redhot razory shrapnel.
At the window, I see nothing.
Correction: I see two girls

playing tennis, they have no
voices, only the muted thump
of the ball kissing the racket,
the sound of a snowball
hitting a snowman, the sound

of a snowman's head rolling
into a river, a snowman with
an alarm clock for a heart
deep inside him. Listen:
someone is breathing.

Someone has a problem
breathing. Someone is blowing
smoke through a straw.
Someone has stopped breathing.
Amazing. Someone broke
his wrist this morning,
broke it into powder.
He did it intentionally.
He had an accident

while breathing. He was exhaling
when his wrist broke.
Actually

it's a woman breathing.
She's not even thinking
about it. She's thinking
about something else.

The Distant Orgasm

I am reading
"'Huh! promising me a hundred children.' Then she
waits for the God to show what he can do, and Siva (but
it can't be Siva) is touched, and forced by her faith,
resuscitates the husband."
And as I am reading
I hear a cry: Ooooooo!
O God, the heart fails
I know it
it can happen next door
(see *Musée des Beaux Arts*)
while you are reading
"What I am telling here is the story according to
the expression of the group. But the Hindus do not know
how to paint, still less how to carve natural expressions.
That is why I am inclined to think that the woman's
attitude should be a little more respectful."
What can I do
but lunge from bed
                    the telephone . . .
no the moments spent
dialing may be her last
the kiss of life
how does it go?
Once I had to try it
on a boy he
was not dying he was
only a cub scout
but he could die
and I could if
I would
save him if
I was not timid
and I was

how *does* it go!
splayed out
in the bathroom she
was stepping
from the shower she
had no history
her heart was free
of history
I would stay with her
hammer the kiss of life
onto her
hold a mirror
over her lips
                Oooooooooo!
She cries again
I am slow closing
the book.
"The Hindu does not rush. He is never elliptic.
He does not stand out from the group. He is the exact
opposite of the climax. He never bowls you over. In
the 125,000 verses of the Ramayanas, in the 250,000 of
the Mahabharata there is not a flash."
I saw her once only
she was not
attractive
no one would call her
beautiful
I hear her music at night
Haydn
she plays when she is alone
as she is most nights
a working woman
up at seven
I hear the alarm
I hear her hum
as the coffee perks
as the bath runs
as the radio
softly conveys the news
that has occurred
in her sleep
and now she is going

she has been called
as my grandmother would say
she is crossing over
as the spiritualiists say
              Ooooooooooo!
a third time she cries
it must be terrible
it did not show mercy
with swiftness
I have heard that cry
I "respond" to that cry
as if it were caught
in my throat
              Ooooooooo yes
she says Oooooooooo yes
I am in the doorway
with one foot raised
the foot stays raised
through the next cry
and the next cry
the foot is becoming
aware of something
the awareness moves
up through the ankle
into the calves
the knees and into the thighs
the thighs say
this neighbor of mine
is not dying
no she is not dying
the foot lowers itself
to the ground
one foot follows the other
back into the bedroom
the hands pick up
the book
the eyes are shy now
they feel foolish
but they must read
to the end.

Someone must think
she is beautiful.

The Private Intrigue of Melancholy

Hotels, hospitals, jails
are homes in yourself you return to
as some do to Garbo movies.

Cities become personal,
particular buildings and addresses:
fallen down every staircase
someone lies dead.

Then the music from windows
writes a lovenote-summons on the air.
And you're infested with angels!

A Guide to the Stone Age

For Charles Simic

A heart that resembles a cave,
a throat of shavings,
an arm with no end and no beginning:

How about that telephone?
—Not yet.

The cave in your skull,
a throat with a crack in it,
a heart that still resembles a cave:

How about the knife?
—Later.

The fire in the cave of your skull,
a beast who died shaving,
a cave with no end and no beginning:

A big ship!
—Shut up.

Instructions which ask you to burn other instructions,
a circle with a crack in it,
a stone with an arm:

A hat?
—Not the hat.

A ship with a knife in it,
a telephone with a hat over it,
a cave with a heart:

The Stone Age?
—There is no end to it.

Wait for Me

A dream of life a dream of birth
a dream of moving
from one world into another

All night dismantling the synapses
unplugging the veins and arteries . . .

Hello I am a cake of soap
dissolving in a warm bath

A train with no windows and no doors
a lover with no eyes for his mask
—inside is the speed of life.

Who can doubt the words of it
each letter written is obsolete
before it finds its friend

Our life is shorter now
full of chaotic numbers
which never complete a day

It will be the same
as it has always been
and you are right to pack

your heart in ice
if you believe this.

The Delicate Riders

I hang my head
on the furniture van
abandoned alongside
an arcaded palace;
alas my woman
is the brand of goose
that cruises through cemeteries
breaking the periscopes
off graves.
I hear a laugh swim up
from the part of myself
I've killed:
those moons
will be there
when I can't even walk.
I know the squalor
of night to night survival,
like the lock of hair
in a dead man's palm.
I place a hanky
over this dream
and wish a trampoline
over her mother's village.
The trees
with their long red hair
dressed in sudden rain
wave a sigh to me—
aphasia smile,
belladonna kiss:
another motionless voyage.
I'll sit down now
and drill a little hole
through this dawnlessness.

If You Would Disappear at Sea

If you would disappear at sea,
if I would ride a horse over the mountains
from Chile to Mexico . . .

No, we are not in the movies.
I cannot promise you
the red wreaths of promise.

Two rooms watching each other.

The door is everywhere and yet
parenthetical, thankless;
so close to home, no way to get there.

We abandon ourselves, become
invisible, blowing over this

charred field, proud
that we have finished with
the pure amateur's
defensive circling.

My Girl

Those empty (blind) trains
crossing the Alps
are trying to find you

The Indian sisters
dead six months
dream of you
they envy your blue eyes
which have no coverings

And from a fourth dimension
lost husbands
are winding their way back
to woo you
from your solitary days

No the gravediggers
will never uncover you
the scrolls don't mention you
once

The poor seekers
with their red lanterns
so close at times
are waylaid by birdcalls
thunder drums

Their work is endless
your name a wishbone
caught in their throats

Absences

1

When did you begin your quest?
I'm late now.
Crucial moment before a shave,
the stars are famished.
Pop off my arms,
give them away, no, throw.
Neither possibility
is a possibility:
putrid sludge of veins and arteries.
I play everything backwards
to see how it will be next time,
such a textbook. All

is suddenly quiet: this legend
has only one knife,
the wind is nothing to me,
like a thousand crows,
trips me in my flight of nightness.
Do you want the bones
beneath my eyelid?
I'm late now.

2

I'm free of that little bit of sunshine.
She has killed me with one cold glance.
I sit back now and wait
for an explosion of larks,
but nothing comes.
Some terrible venom in a stare,
I wish I had one.
Not even hot coals
to carry with me
as I watch the last moth leave.
I existed in the wrong hour of dawn,

that kind of beauty
so no miles from anything.

3

The eye wants to sleep
but the head is no mattress.
I break the railroad in two.
All the terrifying endless chaotic detail,
worthless narcoleptic wombats.
A dirty comb in the house
of the recently deceased.
No wound there, what is it then?
We are doing what we should
in the barbershop cortege,
a great deal of boring
& irrelevant information.
His age is not known.

4

In a drunken moment years ago
the hero would be me,
effervescent, welcoming a rattled polka dot
of snow, instead of just sitting here
nervously, twisting a casual wink
into this, in a ditch computing
the future, the dust & the whiteness.
I feel a morbid desire for music.
It comes to zero,
knowing another is near,
a wise man, singing.
Never say drunken angry visionary.
I knit the floating mouth
to the sheep called nobler.

5

People behaving like molecular structures
with pins in them.
This is what feels best,
as if to say you have grown old

to endless slights of hand.
Yes, ashes fall upward.
You are an extremely ordinary man,
a scarf riding the warm cold wind
in a closet of rags
vampires have abandoned.

6

He asked for it.
When a clock dies
no one wakes.
Mirthless portals
without moisture.
My dream is a canopy:
if the storm bore malice,
have some tea.
I'm living out a sentence,
trying not to break
the interference of fortune.
Lovers are at a loss now,
surrounded by a brilliant display
representing a palm tree
in fireworks
strangled by curlicues of night;

a mirage of fabulous insects
melting in the ballroom
with the warmth of new love;

and the cigarette in the garden,
watching the cabooseman
toss his handkerchief of salt
into an erotic prairie.

I think I remember myself
poised at the end,

holding something
or pushing something away.
What else could I do?

7

We should all be behind bars.
I am the commuter
no matter how unreachably far away.
Burrowing a tunnel
through the dump,
please erase sleep from this dream.
Not a tear was shed all spring.
The springs grow shorter.
I hold my breath in my hand.
Why do I bother to speak?
Make love to a moose, maybe.
I can imagine a wife
serving dinner
of light bulbs & garbage cans.
How do you like your mashed potatoes?
With pins in them.
Pretty soon I am talking
to the secretary
of her personal secretary,
a faithful wife, in herself,

a jaspered morning.

8

So close I came to you
each moment I was alive:
summer of turnstiles,
unnatural waltzes
with funereal jurors.
In the pink lobby
the abortion got away.
Large soft brown disks.
Now it is quiet in the bar:
no one says to the other,
"It is all one to me,
sexuality & the trucking industry."
Break open ourselves,
but there are not enough selves
to go around.

9

The littlest finger on the left hand
on which so much hangs,
sings his silent serenade.
What are you doing?
Where are you going?
The lightning will sting your eyes.
A particular formation of clouds—
I am not referring to my mother,
the gypsy—is learning to speak:
finer cold I should not have to think.
And now they want back their nothing.
But the few I do have
actually I don't have.

The mattress is disembowelled.
When you call her name, Wanda
falls into a deep sleep,
the littlest finger on her left hand
is mugged by lint.

10

I was confused
then I got used to it
as I got used to whiskers.
The laugh is bitter & forced,
flat as a hungover Sunday school teacher
all beat-up by the blight
of the truth of the night before.
There, apologize, for thinking.
A pinched and brittle smile.
Throw a handful of magic
purple dust in my eyes
so I can see the last straw.
All the time I am afraid
the children from my childhood
will get me, my whistling
hot fantasy: those were great moments
in somebody's life.

I look at the ceiling,
then turn and avert my eyes,

and say exactly what is expected of me:
the days just come to me.

Why aren't you in my way?

11

Where do the words go
when I have done with them?
My mouth should chase them.

The moon in her white nightgown,
the moon in her nightgown of nonchalance,
the warm drawers of the moon:

I don't know what I'm going to do
but it will include the terror
of earrings, earrings in the back seat,

nylons on the tub.

12

I had to move across the street
to get a better perspective.
It feels so good I'm never coming back.
I'm with the graveman in his television
over a missile site in Nebraska.
We treat ourselves
to a pizza; lifelines are concrete
around our last secret.
The center of the earth
is a ravenous magnet,
it's hard work
to keep anything away from it.
In a pile of money
try to fornicate,
she on her knees, etc.
The skydiver rises!
The green ghost
breaks the lamp
filling a common grave,
my only evidence.
All of heaven's little soldiers

enter the rainbow of indifference
& ask to come out
for the purpose of blinding
the fools who pretend they know me.

13

A child plots his life to the end;
and spends the rest of his days
trying to remember the plot.
To the pure everything is rotten.
I could guess myself blue.
Fish me out of a sunny bottle
a pocketful of mumbles:
we should get started on that
jade bridge, autumn juvenilia
cannot wait. We should make
history exciting (jejune speculation).
O blind nurse of autumn,
texture of cork, breath
of flügelhorn. Ah . . . Mister Jelly!

14

Life wrapped up in a shoestring,
as I run from room to room.
It changes me as time goes by.
I drive inward
like a rat;
if you hate what you love
or vice versa,
would you burn down a forest
to kill one bear?
All the brouhaha over our survival,
days like ragas: sir the blips
are approaching, the bloats
are groaning.
A world without alps,
like what we've wanted to do
when nobody was around.
Rife with rising roses,
hosanna savanna.

The air crawling out of the tires.

15

Haggling over the privilege
of sending a rubber stamp to Venus

the rampaging butterflies
cut out Lorca's heart
that has cleaned this planet
in a stolen airplane

I got my chance
very dry and ascetic
idle as a lamb

Tomorrow I will give her
a telescope
with my dates respectively
scratched on each lens

adding a small stone
or taking one away
some in couples
some in threes & fours
populate the desert

16

A small man from another world said:
people live on gloomily,
come in cars or boats
—hubba hubba would you look at—
while driving to the business conference,
totally air-conditioned,
sitting with a false humility
when a tree dies.

An asterisk in the heart,
at the same time
the difference between them
so you can read it in a mirror
because "there ain't nothin'
you ain't heard" including
a few previews of The Thing,

drenching herself
just when I feel
it isn't cinematic sex,
it isn't built up to.
Independent of the universe.

17

Thus the galaxy is inhabited
shouting & dancing around
with my ex-girlfriend, the spy.
We had a big fight one night
because she wouldn't wash her hands
of the blood from a coitus
interruptus midnight phone call.
There never vos sich times.
Then I swiftly pierced my Bible
with an icepick &
slept in a field of general blur.
Some particularly dear friend
I can't conceive of
that brings your face to mine,

a well to be filled with
tossed pennies, a pair
of green bikini panties
stranded on the doorknob

is my favorite cave.

18

I have nothing to stop my brother:
as I try to predict his next move
a girl is blowing suds out the window.
There must be millions.
A postcard in the mud
tinkles with transparent scripture.
Sunshine came down
on the weird statues
out front the hotel
of three worlds: your bag
of tears is all

you have to empty
before you enter.

On the clerk's lapel spells Roxy.

19

I'll never go that far again.
I'm happy it's over.
What's inside the fiddle in the meadow?
Under the shadow of the hammer
the constant flow
of the great body snatcher
through the chattering streets.
Way back there in the avalanche
following some ship lover
over the horizon
the mean touchiness of creation
hovers unapproachably

like a permanent wink.

20

Toto, I don't think we're in Kansas.
The orange glow of an erased creature
murdered in comfort by mama's ax
flies into the organ.
The voice of the leaf on the neck
poisons the dowry in the yellow kitchen.
Soft Oothoon, after all, dropped
the wood louse overboard
with a sailor's smile.
And eleven elves drop dead
in the basin of gold trousers.
Prayers lie like pale beards
on the street. Nearing an island,
I forget to wave. It is too beautiful
to excite me with the idea
of accessibility.

South End

The challenge is always to find the ultimate
in the ordinary horseshit why bother

to get in a car and pretend you are going
a different place to live each day as if

in ignorance of each other's desires
betrayals are not counted saturday night

when it was real warm read the paper and fell
off early in a hot flea-infested building

one must pass by the simple objects suitcase
coffee cup tennis shoe to take account of

life which passes by I sit here and stare
watch a ball game or tease the crazy kid

sunday afternoons are worse everything is
closed nobody drops in they all have

families and places to go so I walk
a straight line from this chair to

that table so what I paid fifteen dollars
for that table the dues and still

I'm foiled in every dream some folks
sit out on the front stoop all night

slowly they roll through the dead plum
trees and fill the air with a numbing moan.

My Great Great Etc.
Uncle Patrick Henry

There's a fortune to be made in just about everything
in this country, somebody's father had to invent
everything—baby food, tractors, rat poisoning.
My family's obviously done nothing since the beginning
of time. They invented poverty and bad taste
and getting by and taking it from the boss.
O my mother goes around chewing her nails and
spitting them in a jar: You shouldn't be ashamed
of yourself she says, think of your family.
My family I say what have they ever done but
paint by numbers the most absurd and disgusting scenes
of plastic squalor and human degradation.
Well then think of your great great etc. Uncle
Patrick Henry.

Deaf Girl Playing

This is where I once saw a deaf girl playing in a field.
Because I did not know how to approach her without startling
her, or how I would explain my presence, I hid. I felt
so disgusting, I might as well have raped the child, a grown
man on his belly in a field watching a deaf girl play.
My suit was stained by the grass and I was an hour late
for dinner. I was forced to discard my suit for lack of
a reasonable explanation to my wife, a hundred dollar suit!
We're not rich people, not at all. So there I was, left
to my wool suit in the heat of summer, soaked through by
noon each day. I was an embarrassment to the entire firm:
it is not good for the morale of the fellow worker to flaunt
one's poverty. After several weeks of crippling tension,
my superior finally called me into his office. Rather than
humiliate myself by telling him the truth, I told him I
would wear whatever damned suit I pleased, a suit of armor
if I fancied. It was the first time I had challenged his
authority. And it was the last. I was dismissed. Given
my pay. On the way home I thought, I'll tell her the truth,
yes, why not! Tell her the simple truth, she'll love me
for it. What a touching story. Well, I didn't. I don't
know what happened, a loss of courage, I suppose. I told
her a mistake I had made had cost the company several
thousand dollars, and that, not only was I dismissed, I
would also somehow have to find the money to repay them
the sum of my error. She wept, she beat me, she accused
me of everything from malice to impotency. I helped her
pack and drove her to the bus station. It was too late to
explain. She would never believe me now. How cold the
house was without her. How silent. Each plate I dropped
was like tearing the very flesh from a living animal. When
all were shattered, I knelt in a corner and tried to imagine
what I would say to her, the girl in the field. What could
I say? No utterance could ever reach her. Like a thief

I move through the velvet darkness, nailing my sign
on tree and fence and billboard. DEAF GIRL PLAYING. It is
having its effect. Listen. In slippers and housecoats
more and more men will leave their sleeping wives' sides:
tac tac tac: DEAF GIRL PLAYING: tac tac tac: another
DEAF GIRL PLAYING. No one speaks of anything but nails
and her amazing linen.

First Lesson

This is a meditation:
a snake with legs,
a one-legged snake,
a snake with wings,
a one-winged snake,
a rat with sparks,
a fiery rat,
a rat that sings,
a star rat,
a horse that explodes,
an atomic horse,
a horse that melts,
an ice horse,
a bee that flies through concrete,
a pneumatic bee,
a bee that lifts buildings,
the world's strongest bee,
a tree that eats the noses off children,
a bad tree,
a tree that grows inward until it is a dot,
a hill of dots that eats lots of children
(you are not meditating).

The Soup of Venus

This soup is cold
and it needs something
you probably didn't follow
the recipe, you were
in a hurry and wanted
to surprise me.
That was sweet of you
but you forgot
that I don't like
cold soup.
You might try adding
one bay leaf
while you are in there.
The salt is on the table
and I will experiment
with that myself.
The parsley doesn't
taste much but it
does improve
the appearance.
You used to make
such good soup.
I always bragged
about your soup.
I think that's what
originally attracted me
to you, that hot soup
you used to make.
I loved that soup.
Do you still have
that recipe?
Well this tastes
a little better now,
lukewarm soup
is my second favorite.

The Immortals

None of us have felt good this year:
pus around the eyes,
sores that come and go with no explanation.
But we still believe we will come through it!
I signal this news
by lifting a little finger.

Teaching the Ape to Write Poems

They didn't have much trouble
teaching the ape to write poems:
first they strapped him into the chair,
then tied the pencil around his hand
(the paper had already been nailed down).
Then Dr. Bluespire leaned over his shoulder
and whispered into his ear:
"You look like a god sitting there.
Why don't you try writing something?"

Man with Wooden Leg
Escapes Prison

Man with wooden leg escapes prison. He's caught.
They take his wooden leg away from him. Each day
he must cross a large hill and swim a wide river
to get to the field where he must work all day on
one leg. This goes on for a year. At the Christmas
Party they give him back his leg. Now he doesn't
want it. His escape is all planned. It requires
only one leg.

Saint John of the Cross in Prison

Browsing among the zero hours,
and where I went from there . .
diabolical? No. I went out
of myself into . . . I did not go
out of myself into the after-

noon of parrots; I did not go out
of myself into the dew; I did
not go out of myself into the
bat-terrors. I did not say silence,
I said nothing about the love I

did not go out of myself into.
I said nothing fire, I said nothing
water, I said nothing air. I went
out of myself into no, into
nowhere. I was not alone.

Cycle of Dust

1

Brushfires all around;
I always say that is living.

And stop abruptly to stare
in terror
at the block of ice.

The tentative colors
shrink inward,
a lilac is stuffed into the air;

the last leaves of night
are ripped out
of this blind world

by a still breeze.

2

The strollers are one
unending stroller

all Spring on the tip
of a budless branch

They drink slumped over
in the dark
grazing the cold teeth
of the chisel

Then you are no virgin

a little maple leaf
on a chain

sparkles his stardust
on a stranger

3

Men get down on their knees
and search the toy river

it is daytime
the carnation is bubbling

the owls are sleeping
on a distant black planet

A scarf is pulled quickly
through the veins

of a covered bridge

4

Feeding those pigeons
each spoonful of stone

eyes of a doe
when nobody was around
say in an empty subway
after midnight

like a baby on fire

kicked off the edge

to indicate
there was no sign
or wise man singing

a buoy of blood
is tossed
to the far shore

5

Little hands were sprouting
in the cracks
of the sidewalk

they have been told nothing

a champion of kisses
somewhere writing
my own filthy epitaph

that famous
limp grey ray
of light

jackknifes midword
into a world without alps

but I have no feathers, he said

6

When you put on your nightgown
to get off the ground
the smoke twirls

in amber telephones

Chiaroscuro of fossils
and diving birds

the way I run
from their embrace

into a foreign political paper
tattoed
on a false virgin's cunt

The bazookaman chimed
the first kite of
the day—blindfold the birds

in slippers of secondhands

7

How it will be next time
on the corner
of asylum street

a woman draped over a balcony
in the sky

a poor fiery
oasis
like the candle revealed

in an autopsy
where the vegetables

cry out
on wolf pit road

in the vertebrae of
her bright malaise

the night was clocked
bodies became
covered with dust

they looked like statues

8

With a bloody eye
the egg slid from memory:

don't drop your tooth
in the delta,
old evil dead over there.

Change of chair was
an illusion,

pins in them,
as if to say
they are building a guitar

with strings of milk
for the dog to practice
in his whiskey—

from here to there
I'll never go

destroying the desert

9
Afternoon with a random
stranger in a random

taxi gone down
the drain
in his bathtub,

solitude unfurls
his ribbon

of black light
with the same

savage smile,

perfumed snatches
of a neighbor's party
before

the imaginary
swimming pool,
beneath which

a solitary maggot
the keeper of the keeper

no nothing nothing
at the mercy

of invisible ink.

V

from Hottentot Ossuary

(1 9 7 4)

Waking

I looked grotesque, covered with lice and strange purple roses. A hot bath would be just the thing! I was generous with patchouli bath-oils, tossed in a brand new sponge from the Indian Ocean. I slithered to its edge like a voluptuous serpent. Abandoning myself, I leapt in a high arch, beautiful form throughout the entire movement. To my great astonishment there seemed to be no bottom to this damned tub! I entered the scalding waters like a fresh torpedo, arms stretched, head tucked, feet swept smoothly back: slowly I spent my force, glided for some minutes like a shark after a full meal in sleepy waters.

I dried myself vigorously. Then, with considerable strain, I lifted the tortoise-shell comb which had grown enormous overnight, to my head perched high on the flagpole of my neck. If I'd had any hair left the crush of the comb might have been softened. As it was, I was split perfectly down the middle, nose, naval and penis in equal servings. I felt like a deer chasing a mirage.

There was a taste of honey on the razor blade, honey that sucks bees.

Deadlines

Where are the heroes of the rain? There's a live one carrying a dead one in his mouth, that's very tough work. It seems to me his feathers have gathered too much dust. He doesn't have any idea where he's going to put it. Ah, for the days of robust anarchy! A driving chaos! He staggers into the corner. Trapped, he climbs the wall. The very same wall once walked through the sunken keys of the universe, all headlines contained in his veins. That's nearly impossible, isn't it? Beneath each hawthorn tree sits Nathaniel Hawthorne. I've never seen a live one climb a wall with a dead one in its mouth. Is that true? No! Well, now he's tuckered out, that really took it out of him. It is the American twilight, and some child is reading The Book of Records with a tear in his eye. He puts the dead one down, walks around of course of course in circle in circle he walks around in circles of course of course in circle. I killed the dead one and now of course of course I am going to kill that crazy live one.

Leaping Woman

The leaping woman arrives in an ambulance of starlight. A harness of wet pins shoots through the pure whiteness of her foaming team of white Cadillacs, white hounds in a lost pool of whitenesses. An arm from a window touches half-a-moon; silhouetted aerials switching the night into miracles, miracles of green fiery air, of locomotion and lullaby. Hammer of gigantic thrills. O spew, circle her brilliant black curls! Ash, marble, flame, O detective hummingbird: She's filled with the desire to stand absolutely still! Just now a messenger arrives in fantastic disarray, irregular movements down the gravel detour of inexcusable flowers. A scented handkerchief rises from his passing, ghostly skiff: And she, on her poet's crutches, over annoyed walls, like a loose needle on the deck of a huge, black ship, she finds the meteor still sizzling quietly, she leaps to ramify, she calms, she forgets the present, fluid wonder, passionate denouncing, upping upping upping the weight to carry, the ragged mile to move, the date to remember, forgetting it again. . . .

The Hostile Philharmonic Orchestra

It was awful. Martha and Joe had not seen one another since graduation. Martha's work had carried her away. Joe had taken his father's place on the assembly line. He liked the work and was able to build himself a small nestegg. He drove a Mustang convertible and drank beer at the bowling alley. Martha had a little efficiency apartment in Philly with three other girls. She exchanged contemporary greeting cards with Joe four or five times a year, though she did not refrain from seeing other boys. Whether or not she secretly hoped Joe would some day pop the question is hard to tell—there was Dave, there was Victor and Bruce. Joe had a piece of land all picked out should he someday acquire a wife: he would build the house himself, he had always been good with his hands and loved hard work. His mother and father worried about him though; he did not have many dates. Would he ever leave home, bring them grandchildren? These were questions that haunted them. So they were understandably proud when they read in the morning paper today about Joe and "an unidentified airline stewardess from Philadelphia . . . committing fornication last night . . . at the Philharmonic." The Orchestra maimed them almost beyond recognition.

VI

from Viper Jazz

(1 9 7 6)

Poem (I Can't Speak for the Wind)

I don't know about the cold.
I am sad without hands.
I can't speak for the wind
which chips away at me.
When pulling a potato, I see only the blue haze.
When riding an escalator, I expect something orthopedic to
    happen.
Sinking in quicksand, I'm a wild appaloosa.
I fly into a rage at the sight of a double-decker bus,
I want to eat my way through the Congo,
I'm a double-agent who tortures himself
and still will not speak.
I don't know about the cold,
But I know what I like I like a tropical madness,
I like to shake the coconuts
and fingerprint the pythons,—
fevers which make the children dance.
I am sad without hands,
I'm very sad without sleeves or pockets.
Winter is coming to this city,
I can't speak for the wind
which chips away at me.

Sensitive Ears

It's a tiny noise
like that of eyeliner being applied
like a twenty-year-old smell coming back
to haunt you in a dream
it's the new house
it must be the old house
only this time it enters
through the ears
what a strange odor!
like an entire New Year's Eve Party
shoved down a laundry chute
like waking up from an automobile accident
twenty years older!
and I keep sleeping in the basement
to get away from it
I'm in the treetops
listening to it circle
and I hear a mule puff its last sigh
I can't shut off this wheezing
there's a noise crouched under that leaf
I'm a flea with a thousand microphones
for eyes.

A Voyage from Stockholm
to Take Advantage of Lower Prices
on the Finnish Island of Åland

Out through the frosty archipelago
card-players, morning beer-drinkers,
parsimonious housewives
and Nick Carter readers:

the derelict bum
seems to have a universe
of oddities folded, wrapped, stashed
in his filthy bag:
his tireless attention
to a thousand scraps of paper.

Someone hums a love song
while the others sleep.
No matter how far he might travel
his secret story is written somewhere,
in the generous air, in the distance.

A little patch of sky between suburbs,
about the size of a football field,
or maybe it's a dusty parkinglot,
sees him waving, and is reminded of;—
and in the distance the distance . . .

Alfonso Lacklustre

The shoe was occupied, kind of a picnic
rented to another living companion.
An excellent raincoat makes the bed.
The belt is not heavy, no heavier than the old man's
sleepy lecture on a handkerchief.
It's already 8 o'clock and she is full.
Her driver's license is only moonshine.
She is comfortable with a difficult word.

Is it kind to be amusing, healthy to be striped?
This is my everyday room, full of trays.
The floorlamps are also fruitbowls.
I can boil coffee on the ceiling.
There is a small, three-legged bench in the corner.
Simple and wild this new pillow.
Yesterday morning, tomorrow morning
are immigrants with one shirt between them.

He has a broken foot and has employed a cane
to stop the bus. Later, he'll use his tie
to stir coffee, proof that one has
sufficient money to enter the town.

In back of the bridge chewing-gum
is permitted to work, hair is slicked back
in church. To believe. To live. To feel.
To sew. To dress. To row. To plant.
To shoe a horse. To tell the future.
To flee! Sure. Certainly. Is there
any sleeper on the train? When is
the next train leaving? I'll take that.
I would like a ballpoint pen.
I would like a postcard.

So sad that she is sick!
I dial the right number I dial the wrong number.
She puts down the receiver she picks it up.
That's all right where's the wastebasket,
when does the game begin,
where can I find a small shop selling chocolates?

Awkward Silence

The trees are sprayed
to give the birds
a slight shock
to avoid unwanted attacks
on the President.

Who was it that first started counting,
the first looter?
the one who stripped the dead
of their souvenirs?

We are breaking through so many illusions,
like some kind of ghost dance!
Nothing passes unmarked,
even the machines gossip.

Two powder puffs are talking
on the veranda
while helicopters mate overhead.
The laboratory of eternal sleep

tied to a cat's tail
suffers the little children to suffer.
A ruined church, a ruined library,—
a hospital wishes it were dead.

The room is bugged,
it sucks off energy.
I don't care for its windows anymore,
as if this piece of earth had the right,

to tear up the darkness in search of night.
It's the days when nothing happens,
not a word is spoken,
those are the ones that can be saved.

A Radical Departure

Bye!

I'm going to a place so thoroughly remote
you'll never hear from me again.

No train ship plane or automobile
has ever pierced its interior

I'm not even certain it's still there
or ever was
the maps are very vague about it
some say here some say there
but most have let the matter drop

Yes of course it requires courage
I'll need two bottles of vintage champagne every day
to keep the morale high

and do you mind if I take your wife?
Well, I guess this is it
we'll see ourselves to the door

Where are we . . . ?

Read the Great Poets

What good is life without music.
But that's impossible,
one shuffle has always led to another.
One man hears it start on his lathe,
a mother beats her eggs.
There's a typewriter in the next room.
Two cars are angry at each other.
The baby downstairs is wet again.
I remember the voice of a dead friend.
Everything speaks at the same time.
Music will watch us drown.

I write letters to all those from whom I receive
and to many of those from whom I don't.
I read books, anything, useless piles of random
insufferable rubbish for which, in my torpid panic,
I fall through time and space each day
in my foolish way, remembering only the present feeling,
not the village with its face of death,
nothing to be carried secretly in a car.
I move from the stiff-backed chair
to the brown leather one
as the day wears on. And then finally
the couch, allowing the spirit to leave
the broken body and wander at will.
Lately it's a pasture of Holsteins she longs for.

There's a certain point in each evening when I have to put on
some really soul-shattering rock-and-roll music and comb my
hair into this special caveman fright-wig. I've done as much as
two or even three dollars worth of damage to my apartment in
one hour of all-stops-pulled Bacchic, Dionysian celebration and
revolution of this great dull life, so fascinating it hypnotizes you
and then puts you to sleep, only to never know the ending. It's

strange though, no one ever complains. Is it what I feared all along? We are playing the same song and no one has ever heard anything.

People read poems like newspapers, look at paintings as though they were excavations in the City Center, listen to music as if it were rush hour condensed. They don't even know who's invaded whom, what's going to be built there (when, if ever). They get home. That's all that matters to them. They get home. They get home alive.

So what it's been burgled. The heirlooms. Mother's rings, father's cufflinks. They go to a distant island and get robbed there. It's the same everywhere. Read the great poets, listen to the great composers. It's the same everywhere. The Masters. The Thieves.

On the Subject of Doctors

I like to see doctors cough.
What kind of human being
would grab all your money
just when you're down?
I'm not saying they enjoy this:
"Sorry, Mr. Rodriguez, that's it,
no hope! You might as well
hand over your wallet." Hell no,
they'd rather be playing golf
and swapping jokes about our feet.

Some of them smoke marijuana
and are alcoholics, and their moral
turpitude is famous: who gets to see
most sex organs in the world? Not
poets. With the hours they keep
they need drugs more than anyone.
Germ city, there's no hope
looking down those fire-engine throats.
They're bound to get sick themselves
sometime; and I happen to be there
myself in a high fever
taking my plastic medicine seriously
with the doctors, who are dying.

Same Tits

It was one of those days. I was walking down the St. and this poster glassed in a theater billboard caught my eye. A really gorgeous set of tits. It was noon, hot as hell outside. So I said what the hell, paid my $2.50 and went in. Got a seat all by myself right in the middle. The curtain opens: there's the same poster by itself in the middle of the stage. I sat there sweating. Finally decided to get the hell out of there. It was still noon, hot as hell outside.

Dry Cup

And you my cone
of hot nickels
my pietà
with a steaming locomotive

       problem child

The pyrotechnics
that bring you back
in the sad form
in the formless sandbox

       without shores

where you're drowning
to hold up your feet
you're dying to show us
something really wet

       and shining

with your sideburns lit up
to show us the meaning
what a flivver
what a brief cameo

       ad for pain.

Village 104

The architecture, sleepy Mexican,
is afraid to go out.
Young couples go there to settle down
and not raise a family.
Retired people open shops
and refuse to sell anything.
It is an easy place to like
without really liking it.
You can get to know
without really knowing it.
It's the invisible that is ruthless.
Sombody is going to grow up
and kill it, make a killing,
so you'll never seem so lonesome.

Marfa

I sent my love to the showers.
My sisters are on the blink.
The beer must take a letter.
These poems are on the house.
Say you miss me, Marf, I'm out of gas.
If this is the information you've been seeking,
I'm a lost and pissed-off alias.
My personal self has not felt your private breasts.
I mean nothing to the circles of mocha.
I was not born there.

I'm consoled by this hole
where you once tarried, a rope
around the wilderness.
You've got me surrounded.
I can't come any closer.
I crawl inside you like a car.

Is it true that we are fools
to have ever expected
anything else?
Just once we should have been
staring at one another
over candlelight and cognac
in a Grand Hotel anywhere.
Two people can build one fast
in emergency situations
which have been the only ones
dealt us thus far.
But we couldn't even afford the poverty.

Marfa, I'm still locked up in jail
with boxcars on my mind.
Marfa, today I'm so happy all this is falling apart.
I give my purse strings a tug

and drive on through the grove.
Saw my hand shrivel.
Saw rags swim across the sky.
I dreamed I was home, and that I had left,
I had even left the leaving, so far back was this
I was supposed to be home thirty years ago.
My wife will think I don't love her.
My beautiful wife!
Or was it my mother?

You've gone walking on the mountain alone.
There was much sadness in your face.
I've hurt you again over the price of cheese.
Without you, the calm is delirious.
Perhaps up there you can look down on me and laugh.
Marfa has nothing, she is pure spirit up there.
(I could say something nice about her now that she is gone:
She has perfect teeth. And not only that
                                        she rules the world.)

                Wall of death edumacation
                    booky booky
                manic blue flowers
                        for
                    Marfa
                    silver flowers
                    silver flowers for Marfa
                    the wall of death
                    stack my deck
                    for Marfa
                Manic blue flowers.

Amherst to Easthampton

I ain't got no body
seizing my spirit.
My spiritual body has no body.
My body has no body,
and my spirit hath no spirit.
like the like the like the like the
nest of spiders beneath your arms,
the wind carries your shadow through her dark hills.

The darkness you cast off seeks me,
eats a hole through the chocolate forest that separates us,
empty spaces filled with a fine down.

The Glassy Harbor

O faint sad noises
and milky dullness,

rose-colored blindness
in evening gowns

how moist and rhythmic
those who walk near

the glassy harbor.
Silent drift of deserters

from the theater,
and everywhere the stars

receding, receding . . .
nothing to hold onto

but their own silver hearts.

"Dreamy Cars Graze on the Dewy Boulevard"

Dreamy cars graze on the dewy boulevard.
Darkness is more of a feeling inside the drivers.
The city is welded together
out of hope and despair.
The seasons pass imperceptibly,
more of a feeling inside the streetcleaners:

"Come quick, Hans,
a leaf is falling inside of me!"

Bug Sleep

The bugs' sleep is full of lead,
full of love for the earth.
Sprawled out like body surfers,

dark little angels,

can they hear a tapping on the floor?

And when the bugs' sleep is loosed
at sunrise

it flies into the trees
and perches there
like the shining-back of golden moments.

Autumn

The transference bird of little mind has risen high
by its wings of coincidence
in the spacious sphere
of ineffable radiant light
in the lamasery of Pullahari
in the lamasery of non-dual carburetors

In the offering pit of the apparitional body
the fuel of evil tendencies of normal forms
the fuel of dream tendencies
that have been heated up
in the lamasery of the sharp knife
a heavenly tree with which the corpse fans himself.

Poem

Language was almost impossible in those days
as we know it now and then.

When you tell me about your operation
I hear you, but I don't hear you.

Wind gathers behind a barn:
torches are lit, men whisper.

One wears a hat and is very serious
about the war in his bedroom.

"Does it seem like I am sleeping all the time?"
Ask me another question.

Look, Ma, I found something beautiful today
out in the forest, it's still alive . . .

In a Motel on Lake Erie

Tequila & chicken
causing lunar distress.
Nothing promising
on the tb—one symphony
of skeletons, two
black dots, one mountebank
of incurable disease,
one rainbow ground into
dog-ticks. Oh, it is dark here.
I can hear squeaks, probably
elephants. I try to call
the cops but they're
at the ballgame, a benefit
for those who can see.
I turn the lights on in my skull—
what a beautiful evening!
It is like a tombstone
full of vital information.
The highway eagles now
living out this dream.

A Dime Found in the Snow

Tomorrow the future will be here,
open her great droopy eye.
She will clean out the barn
with a white boa thrown round her neck
while the pterodactyl dreams
in his floral chambers, destitute
of feathers and the supporting surface
of wings, dreams of the difference
between a long time and a short time,
of getting out of this life
and staying—a flower and a fire engine,
out of this world. Miss Future
might remember something, some summer,

but she's tired and anxious
for a new oblivion, something
to agitate her. Just for the hell of it
she has the ball on the lawn
roll away from home. The opponent,
her father, takes advantage of this
situation, this holiday, and pours
a flame through her yawning hoop,
a red nothing, one of everything.
And, with spite for tomorrow's sameness,
makes the wild river quiet inside.
With all her sex she turns away
from this possible unnatural temple

of transmogrified instants,
and throws a few gravestones
at her children, asleep in manicured
detachment, in an airplane that floats
like a song, in a Cadillac full
of roses (that stalls on the beach),

and on seahorses that back
into their twinkling caves;
an inclination to cling to them,
to not let them slip, to let them sleep—
an icicle that grows from a tree,
a feather thrown into a canyon,
a dime found in the snow.

VII

from Riven Doggeries

(1 9 7 9)

Riven Doggeries

A miserable day, his dog had leapt
from the window
The dog had leapt
from my seventh-story apartment
into a Police helicopter
that had been hijacked
by some well-meaning murderers.
But it was for dogs
they entertained no mercy.
And that afternoon, late, after
a cold shower I went
for a ride in our elevator,
an immaculate dive, home
of the lost soul and once third base
to late working things.
My animal has sunk
he doesn't exist
he won't come back.
The ideal pet, however,
is unrecognizable when it arrives
in the river awash in the land afar.

Heatstroke

I always have many flowers—
my neighbor gives them to me.
I seem not to have the strength
to go on with my confession.

That beautiful woman is a Chilean:
she is a fickle woman, an intelligent
good woman, very beautiful. That is
the trouble: I never have the correct

time. You see the sense this is making,
the old Presidential Palace? Always
she is tending the garden with loving
excellence—in one motion, everything

at stake for that instant. Some star
fell down on her and so what.
But it's not as always, the fickle woman
does not die at the hands of her lover;

many sharing an idea of beauty, beauty
a necessity in every breathful—this is
what she is saying. But it's not
as always; and if not that need

then another, half-visible, on an errand,
swept along, shape and shadow: use me
and be done with it; tear them down
and build them up—it's one motion.

Look back, what life has become: the sky
is clearly alien, amazement,
star of my night blasts the subtle shifts
of mood. She is my desperate angel

so why expect anyone to believe,
to keep the myth squeezing itself,
the most sensible of savage choices:
Her soul in its misfire knocked once,

an indelible stamp.

Rooster

Tomorrow, since I have so few,
and Tomorrow, less dramatically,
and Tomorrow any number of times.
As for renouncing, isn't that
the oldest?

Rooster crowing: dark blue velvet
that knows itself too well—
empty wallet, busted heart—
Oh yes, my very good friend,
a voice searching for orchids,
that dances alone.

And then for that one hour
there are no familiar faces:
this lovely, misbegotten animal
created from odd bits of refuse
from minute to minute
splits us down the middle.

Sloops in the Bay

The sloops in the bay are talking in a little bottle
language, their laughter
is the most difficult number in the book,

a sweeping, a rolling
like the bilious voyage of sleep—

They are starting to burn
like the yellow leaves at the bottom of a dream.

They can't sleep now, it would be quite impossible.
Whispering like a garden of secrets.

With a Child All Day

Little ragamuffin, brat, a craving for Sen-Sen
as we walked along the Académie;
it is all that interests you.
I remain quiet and my manner annoys you;
I'm present and unaccounted for.
The tunnels are not crowded in this part of the city.

Finally I say I like dogs, possible dogs, worn thin.

We're in the wrong place, our favorite season.
Ill luck has surfaced again and you do as you please.
I hang on to you around the corner.
There is something lacking even now.
Come, whitewash my fasting worth.

Something living touched me; a plant?
You pretend to recognize old friends.
Why this embarrassed despair, this recoiling?
City of Love—I can't breathe.

Our own God gave us, gave us the bird.

Goodbye.

Nature Poem: Demanding Stiff Sentences

We wanted something: a nude instance
of gaga, a tern in a sunken hammock,
anecdotes that end with angry pigeons,
pinochle won. Should think profound—

profound was the wrong word. We won't
get anything so don't expect anything,
a babe in the mouth and knees sacked
dandling the natal muse, the hysterical

victim's bouquet in Springtime. But we
wanted something more than a fire's embrace
and a worker's trance. We wanted one wail
that would benefit the whole adventure

or a last nickel to call home and thank ma.
Geography, now there's a short street—
the buildings, the great outdoors (which remain
just that) flirtatious as blood-donors—

why, I don't know—who sleep by the fountain
in the shade of the palm. They didn't know
the first thing about fishing, which was their
lifelong ambition. Rivers, like churches full
of bawdy ballads, the keen sloth greeted
by scrappy doves raving in the sky.
And fish, the furniture of fish, talked back.
Typos in a U-boat, we were all members
of Nature's alphabet. But we wanted more.

Time X

His clock has stopped watching.
His watch, an immense presence,
an octopus with jewels.

His clock stops about twice a year
in private and for about three months.
The rest of the time it goes on doing its business
"awake to its time and place" and so on.

But for now his clock has stopped watching,
his back-up band is dead.

His television has rabies,
the bake-sale is canceled.
No more Rembrandt-phonebill.
He's too depressed to vote.

The room, much later,
and the room still later,
and then finally inevitably
the death of the room.
O room, to have stopped running,
you wild home!

The Shy One

Don't look at me
splintering these daffodils,
when I'm at my worst
defoliating their atoms:
I'm one of the hideously weak sort,
a silhouette that roosts
on a streetlamp and
murmurs a low fire.

Of course I sometimes blame it
on the circumstances
of my unholy birth,
hanging there, a stranger
torn by solitary comets:
How could I see beyond
that somber spark?

I spoke words on a banjo
swooning in mint sauce,
heard dulcimer squalls
in my hot suite.
If I could sing like poultry
with flaming green lips
wag my head through perfume,
I would be pleased
as a tipster nomad
in his bath. Alone and proud,

proud cloud poised above my wrist
and cruel chords remembering . . .
And because of this
and so much more, I am allowed
to scratch my way to the surface again:
A fabulous homing instinct remains,
and wounds.

The Life of Poetry

This is how I bend over backward
to tie my shoes, I blink
across the night romancandle.
An omnibuzz, like typing on my tongue.
I want to sleep on these blank pages.

I shake this match and it won't go out,
a kamikaze blown in on a breeze.
I can't sleep brushing you.
Unbone my hand, early warning.
Unbone this cloud, possible showers.

Self is to be commended for correct
adult deportment at self's recent funeral
(except for ignoring the no-smoking sign).
Pass the sweet, Salty, it is morning:
the streets are tilted and rocky,

a newborn foundling has pinned its mother
with barely a whimper—Can't we discuss this
on the phone? A shot is fired next door,
miss the cat? Will those few
please sit up and speak to me;

otherwise I'm forced to conclude *keep walking,*
what's at the core of it, keep walking.

River's Story

There was a boy named river
got up one day on the right side of bed
so he ran up to the lake
and said excuse, have I lost my way?
Lake did not speak English.
River stood there with his pants down
pissing right into the lake.
Lake didn't even care, lake
is still lake, river still river

The next day river got up on the wrong side of bed,
river leapt up, reaching around to snap his spine,
that felt good, now watch this—through the forest
in a wild chase for life, stops at an unlikely cabin,
gets his hide tanned for waking the lazy minister,
and also the visiting coalman delivered several exasperating
    punches beneath the child's proud earring.
The world can be a crooked and crazy place for a boy named
    river.

A girl named Veronica Lake had it really good for a while.
Then it got progressively worse
until they had to dredge her main,
they were attempting to actually measure her depth
with hooks the size of a giant, an aberrant of say 12 stories.
But river's story was just a teardrop, a dewdrop the size of
Chicago and all its vast prairie of concrete.

The Responsible Romance

I stood there on the bridge and watched the moonbeams varnish the smirking crocodiles. Now and again one of them slid from the mud and ghoulishly passed beneath me like an iceberg on the prowl. I was a feverish swindler in edible birds' nests with a muted interest in guano. With my clawed valise and rugged charm I traveled the islands, stopping in dumpy hotels in search of fortune, frowning my way through monsoon or lurking in muffled teak forests. Some day I'd end up on a slab of marble in Auckland, a mustard seed clutched in my fist, foiled at last in my own perishable rhapsody. The damage done but no one to call it folly.

Far off now I hear drumming, then a wail, twangings of an extinct instrument. Footfalls. That face, I know it: it is the class president from my high school. What does he want of me now, in this infernal jungle, nine thousand miles and twenty-five years from that poisonous fenced-in playground for imbeciles.

He was puffing and frothing in his lawyer's garb: "You must come, we need you . . ." I flung my cigarette into the river, a crimson knot of hope against such stammering accidents as this. And yet, what good is it. Already rasping machines are turning my life into a twenty-five word account. *It's none of your beeswax,* I wanted to say. Instead, slipping into something comfortable, I made haste, stumbled and bluntly accepted the call, the signal from the pit, to return to my nook in the deaf opulence of fossils mending their clocks.

Goodtime Jesus

Jesus got up one day a little later than usual. He had been dreaming so deep there was nothing left in his head. What was it? A nightmare, dead bodies walking all around him, eyes rolled back, skin falling off. But he wasn't afraid of that. It was a beautiful day. How 'bout some coffee? Don't mind if I do. Take a little ride on my donkey, I love that donkey. Hell, I love everybody.

In the Realm of the Ignition

Just for this afternoon
the traffic patterns polish the primordial ways,
so that thinking this thought is almost
like driving home, kind of numb all over.
I am so crusty and rusty and dusty from driving
the obvious ramp, that safe and silly sort-of drifting
toward a state of perfect adjustment
and not thinking about a thing.
These are simply flawed traffic patterns,
and these cars are driven into the next century
like satisfied impermanent pigs,
and in their stately mission
they are only getting older.

The cloverleaves are folding.
There is an X on this window,
almost exquisite, the slight madness,
kiss and forgiveness.

I must turn over a new automobile.
This day reminds me
of all the others, and the virgin
lanes looming just out of reach,
the particular gaping maw of this day
dripping in slow or no motion
like a nocount accountant taxing himself beyond reason,
strictly speaking in the tollhouse of grief
like smoke joining the World Sensorium for just a moment.
Aug! The One! This new power is very great!
I must buy one of these new automobiles,

upward and away!

VIII

from Constant Defender

(1 9 8 3)

Land of Little Sticks, 1945

Where the wife is scouring the frying pan
and the husband is leaning up against the barn.
Where the boychild is pumping water into a bucket
and the girl is chasing a spotted dog.

And the sky churns on the horizon.
A town by the name of Pleasantville has disappeared.
And now the horses begin to shift and whinny,
and the chickens roost, keep looking this way and that.
At this moment something is not quite right.

The boy trundles through the kitchen, spilling water.
His mother removes several pies from the oven, shouts at him.
The girlchild sits down by the fence to stare at the horses.
And the man is just as he was, eyes closed, forehead
against his forearm, leaning up against the barn.

Poem for the Sandman

The child begins to walk
toward her own private sleeping place.
In the pocket of her bathrobe
she clinches a hand grenade.
She is lumbering through the lumberyard
like a titmouse with goosebumps.
She waves goodbye to the orthodox dart games.
The noodle shops have returned
to their antholes, gulp, and a single spoor
has traveled all the way from Wichita
to tuck her in and tell her a story.
There, at a juvenile crossroads,
livestock are dragging their saliva
in a semicircle, it is like pulling taffy.
The child stands there for a moment,
sees herself as an ancient washerwoman
playing bingo on Saturday nights.
She, the child, is counting lemons
and squirming before a quiz.
She is standing in a vestibule,
an airless, gravelly vestibule,
when a hearse pulls up and offers her a lift.
Audibly aching, she swerves to miss
some typhoid victims (being shampooed by
an uncle on furlough?) (who pampers her
with infinitesimal sighs?) and bounces
into bed at last as into a cedar bough.
And the sandman stops playing pinball
to mend her cocoon, to rinse her shroud.
He has had his eye out for her all along.
Her tired little soul could not survive another war.

Five Years Old

Stars fell all night.
The iceman had been very generous that day
with his chips and slivers.

And I buried my pouch of jewels
inside a stone casket under the porch,
their beauty saved for another world.

And then my sister came home
and I threw a dart through her cheek
and cried all night,

so much did I worship her.

The Horseshoe

I can't read the small print in the scrapbook:
does this say, *Relinquishing all bats, feeling faint
on the balcony?* There is so much to be corrected here,
so many scribbles and grumbles, blind premonitions.
How does one interpret, on this late branch, the unexpected?

I can see just here that strength was gathering, perhaps
even an excess, and, specifically, the heart-rending detail
of the horseshoe found propped against the windowsill.
Years of toil to find the right angle, I'm almost rigid
with anticipation, maneuvering as at an opera intermission.

Stropping the razor, occasional whining, exploits of idleness—
all are clenched against a teatime eventuality, the progenitors
with their inspired plaintive skeletons engulf us here
for several pages, then sink, like migrating hooves.
What happened to them? I trusted their wings, their
heroic gusto methods. I am shaving this gossipy impetus

like rigid articles away from my face. I see the corrections
penciled in, I'm privy to their forgetfulness, a sprawling
design: I look away and project streaks of hesitant chance
wherever I look. Pulsating veins of thin planks to help me
bridge this muscular aria. Aslant the tone of Life's dialogue,

between siestas, the horseshoe diversion is polished, its legs
degenerating, athletically anyway. It's all in the ankle
or the wind, in breeding bones. Scrapbook, I am in the middle
of your hive, I must take back your corrections to the mute
and infirm stretches of my own big shave, swell the parallel
world with your murky burden, still betting against this charm

nailed to the sidedoor of a photograph to ward off, what was it,
was it me?

The Wild Cheese

A head of cheese raised by wolves
or mushrooms
recently rolled into
the village, it
could neither talk nor
walk upright.

Small snarling boys ran
circles around it;
and just as they began
throwing stones, the Mayor
appeared and dispersed them.

He took the poor ignorant
head of cheese home,
and his wife scrubbed it
all afternoon before
cutting it with a knife
and serving it after dinner.

The guests were delighted
and exclaimed far into the night,
"That certainly was a wild cheese!"

Nobody's Business

The telegram arrived
and no one was there to read it.
The hens shooed themselves from the porch,
softly, with tentative pleas for rainwater.
Inside, the house stiffened, halted in mid-flight.
On its nail an apron flapped, then froze.
And in the hallway, slippers fidgeted, then stood
dazed like questionable theatrical props
on the stairs. A suitcase wiped its brow:
so this is the last stop and no one
is here to meet me.

The journey was withdrawn at the last minute:
the footbridge ached now, felt sticky all over.
The station was deserted, and a sweetness like medicine
sculpted the air with numb monosyllables.

Spacious recesses tried imitating a troupe of mimes,
but it was not fair to the exits: they clustered
in a private booth and shakily came to this conclusion:
resources would have to be pooled for the purchase
of a kitten, surely a marginal concession
to the concentration of this new displeasure.

And so, piercing the cold interior, she came
like money into an early morning poker game.
Tousled the shaky ego of the home.
She was the inevitable passenger
who, within days, shriveled into an uncanny submission,
found an alcove in the world and merged
with the unhealthy halting rhythm.

A child with his birthday telescope
has observed all this. He tells no one,
it is nobody's business. But nothing is forgotten.
Clad only in fluid intervals, he is untouchable,
mincing toward that housewarming
that is surely his.

Tell Them   Was Here

I got there on time
and no one was home.
I waited, paced the sidewalk.

I looked at my watch and shook
my head: Where are they?
I went around back and peered
into the windows: no life.

Unreliable ancestors!
Then it was night and I began
to doubt: It's all lies,
I came from no one, nowhere,
had no folks and no hometown,

no old friends. I was born
of rumors, a whisper in one
state, an unsubstantiated brawl
in another, uncontiguous state.

Green was here, I scrawled
on a scrap of paper, and stuck it
inside the screen. Started to leave,

turned, scratched out my name—
then wrote it back again.

Spring Was Begging to Be Born

After a winter of seclusion
I curtsy farewell to my pagoda:
Friend, tinfoil gangster, deviant silo,
I leave you to your own stale resources
to wander this spring in my disguises,
in my new naked zigzagging across
the pulsating battlefields of my own kind.

*

Murmur of cherry blossoms, I winced, glassy-eyed:
Had not I dreamed their color in my fairy tale?
Then hush; homeless now, I am arriving
at my one true home, the barricades melting.
The further I delved into these murderous zones
the more crisscrossed and woven became
the life within my fussy warehouse and that
beside this celebrated outer cherry.

*

Your wish is my command, I said to no one special.
Feeling festive now, and somewhat fraudulent,
I waited for the zodiac to sneak a glance
at my horoscope. Was this to be, spluttering,
with the plumes of raspberry light
erasing my hearsay and stifling my double?
I picked a thread from the zillion squiggles
and followed it around the corner to where
an orchestra was looking askance and
asking for complete silence.

*

Men sat outside their factories playing dominoes.
Their bodies were swollen, as after a hurricane.
I had dreamed of this hour; and yet, standing there,
my dream seemed suddenly, monotonously, attenuated,
as though a tugboat were the wiser to ignore

this sinking ship. I moved on, sobbing, giggling,
and looked back more than once to no hands waving.
Spring was truly begging to be born
like a cipher that aspires to the number one.
Hush. It is all hearsay, irresistible hearsay.

Mystic Moment

I faced the Star Maker, the candy butcher
from the window of a Pullman car
just outside Pueblo, Colorado,
from a plush and velvet world
with plugs of tobacco
outside a jelly factory.
The vibration of names, a cardinal—
Behind me, Gabriel.
Rounded up like rats
on Metacombie Kay.

First leap at Little Steel,
and the invaders vacuumed
with a ferocity of elegance
seldom encountered, and never
in circles or indifferently.
The Sante Fe Railroad was really something in those days.

The mountains had long ago crumbled away,
erased by some soft artillery on the radio.
I thought I saw my twin, limbless on the desert,
drowning near a herd of angels; I reached out the window
and killed him with a single blow.

The momentousness of the moment demanded it:
there were organs in the post office
and weapons in the organs.
The angels signaled for pandemonium
and soon I was engulfed with temptations,
I was invested with contact with
the populous interiors of many dying stellar worlds.

I faced the Star Maker, the candy butcher,
swarms of burnt-out stars,
from the window of a Pullman car.

Yonder

Look yonder at winding boy
surrounded by the three azure-eyed
flower-weaving daughters
(under every flower a serpent coiled).

They are like liana vines
around a palmetto.

They ply their shuttles in the roaring loom
of time, in the inaccessible regions.

And when they die their web is left
unfinished.

Winding boy insisted: "Hurting is not
my profession."

Yonder winding boy volunteered
to walk them home in the evening.

Then a bulldozer came down the pike,
and then a psychiatrist covered with lice.

Winding boy and the remaining daughters
exchanged niceties and the World-Egg

and dentistry. There are many words
on the tongues of the ineffable,
to clash their cymbals before the cavern of night.

They direct the sound, the sound which
"goes out into all worlds," for their god
is a twisted dragon, a certain spiral force.

Yonder winding boy and the Marvels
their dusty vocal cords.

Beyond that, there is a void, an office,
where they are waiting to get their hearing
at the bar of history itself, succinct and factual.

One of them says: "If I regret anything,
I regret this."

Summer Night

"If you raise canary birds," my grandfather said to me,
"feed them birdseed." Indeed, it is certain disaster
to not give them water as well, I figured out for myself.
And sonic booms will give them a headache, they have no taste

for coffee. "No, Zosine," I moaned softly, "no, Zosine."
Long after his death, one man arose to defend his memory.
Unfortunately, that man's character and writings made him
certain to do more harm than good. Brittle stars,

sea lilies, I sit here at the window and gaze back at the waiters
on the kitchen porch of the Chinese restaurant, getting cool
after a hot spell. They don't know how to interpret what
    they see,
dinosaurs two feet long, worms thirty feet long, a one-ton

jellyfish. "Must they not have terrible, cold hearts,"
Zosine again whispered, "to figure out everything like that?
And to go on, day by day, carrying out their scheme."
I longed for the gift to shake loose rain, but only briefly.

Variations, pigments: next door the painted lady and the red
admiral, the spangled fritillary, cannonsmoke and sewing
    machine.
My grandfather also said, "The brightness of the colors is said
to depend upon the emotions of the insect. What a beautiful way

to express one's feelings, to be able to glow like melted gold
when one is happy." He obviously did not want to take
his own business seriously, but all the same his voice had
    changed.
The Lion hath not prevailed. To open the book, and to loose

the seven seals thereof (to judge every one according to his
    state):
the wings of the male are velvety black and those of the female
are smoky in color, with a distinct white stigmata spot on the tip
of each wing. Common as Tasmanian grasshoppers. Common

task, water. Dreadful fantasies chattered, laughed. Metallic
black, the storm was on the right path. The race of Edwin—
a long, mild, intense glance. Moss animals, labor, hinged
shells. Lake monsters, nobody really knows what to do
    with them.

There is no other name, backboneless. Adults that emerge
during wet weather are frequently darker in color than adults
that emerge during dry weather. Aquatic labor, ribbon-shaped,
coiled. "Nay, Zosine, be quiet," I whispered, "you have been
    dreaming."

"If you are right," said Zosine, "if you are right, if all this
is possible, what are we to do then?"

Nausea, Coincidence

An elderly policeman stands beside my statue of him.
Ah, impersonal, navy-blue, go away.

I am careful to pounce on this wickedness,
this new episode revolving around the teapot.
I have clawed my way into it!
I ceremoniously avoided mentioning my nail file because,
to me, the wiles of its stem
are over there, in the heart of the periphery.

The bar of soap next to the carafe
is getting on my nerves, I am disabled
by the slender blowing of that cucumber
and am forced to hiccup at the reality of my flashlight.
I sense disaster as a wasp flits hieroglyphics on my vision:
I pop him a good pop, insert the corpse into a volume of love
    poems.

Suddenly I feel silly and ill. This apartment
has embarked, it cheeps out of the harbor,
vibrating, groping, with reveries clinging to the hull
it is still more than half empty.
How shallow this peeking, this passage
from the faded perfume of solid ground.
Someone has forgotten his crutch—
now I have placed my hands in my pockets.

Blue Spill

He's been wading deeper into the accident area
where he's the fatherless son and the sonless
father. He walks on through the valley and over
the mountains, some still virgin, with the same
concentration, heart, he has benefited from this

spill. He is now betrothed to blue, at home with
her wisdom of refracted light, troubled only in the
sprinkly dawn, in a blue beret. Blue becomes him;
he was moved as it worked its way up his leg—
was beautiful to behold this sight of blue meeting

blue, why such cause of joy? Thank you turned
into a gaze, blue's aura and dream. It must be
the Aegean, he is swimming in it! O pale body,
he writes this passage for himself to remember . . .
this very special private island was wished

by him, he brought it on by his contact with
illuminated manuscripts, such fingers! Tips
of—guess what—blue, and bluest eyes, this light
is home at last, this blue is blue all through.
He's in control as he strides further into the

meadow, dripping, but he's weathered a lot worse.
Forgive me for not lying about this but he
could be dead right now if he hadn't wandered into
this lucky accident area, where his new life
begins quietly in the eyes of a wakened animal.

Yellow Newspaper and
a Wooden Leg

The children stood watch by the crematorium
since early morning. From my schoolhouse window
I watched, drumming my fingertips, as they squinted
into the sun. A stone's throw away,
a gingko tree would have offered plentiful shade.

The one with thick glasses stared off at the mountain
and a droplet of saliva hung from his chin
far into the afternoon. I hooted and distorted
the image several times, fondled my smock
and chain: It was my luck to hibernate

in a forest fire, to stubbornly tough it out.
When would we know? The baby chicks at the peephole
thought a legend was being burned,
and the ashes were the bottom of that fortune.
They were in the full bloom of their delivery

even as the sun hushed and the damp began its quiver.
They hugged one another, and the corpse yawned,
for a moment sat up. Then, plunging, it seethed
and disappointed, finally cringed hugging itself
blood to ashes, and to a precise, metallic aroma.

Constant Defender

My little finger's stuck in a
Coca-Cola bottle and I've got three
red checkers lodged in my watchpocket.
In a rush to meet my angel, now
I don't even know who my angel was.
I can see seven crimson jeeps lined up
outside Pigboy's Barbecue Shack—
must be a napkin salesmen's convention.
I don't care what cargo as long as
their hats are back on by eleven.
The thing I'm trying to avoid
is talking to my mule about glue futures.
What's a fellow going to do? I must
have a ceiling fan, I can't postpone
twirling blades. And my one stuffed chair
was owned by a hunchback from a hundred years
before I came along. I need some new
knickknacks to suggest an air of cleanliness
to this sluggish pit of extinct sweet potatoes.
Ah, trickery, you sassy lark, withered black pearl,
unfetter me from these latches, make me
the Director at every meatball's burial,
lacerate this too, too static air
I've been eating my way through.
I lunch on eels and larks in lemonade, Lord,
I'm so happy I woke up in my right mind today.
And those kleptomaniacs, Smitty and Bob,
stole peanuts from a hunchback, snuff from an angel.
My knees click, I won't budge, like a wind-up toy
unwound, my guitar held tightly between my thighs.
Last night a clam fell from the stars:
a festive, if slippery occasion, a vibrating blob
entered our midst—I say "ours" out of some need—
I was alone when it hit me.

The Motorcyclists

My cuticles are a mess. Oh honey, by the way,
did you like my new negligee? It's a replica
of one Kim Novak wore in some movie or other.
I wish I had a foot-long chili dog right now.
Do you like fireworks, I mean not just on the 4th
of July, but fireworks any time? There are people
like that, you know. They're like people who like
orchestra music, listen to it any time of day.
Lopsided people, that's what my father calls them.
Me, I'm easy to please. I like ping-pong and bobcats,
shatterproof drinking glasses, the smell of kerosene,
the crunch of carrots. I like caterpillars and
whirlpools, too. What I hate most is being the first
one at the scene of a bad accident.

Do I smell like garlic? Are we still in Kansas?
I once had a chiropractor make a pass at me,
did I ever tell you that? He said that your spine
is happiest when you're snuggling. Sounds kind
of sweet now when I tell you, but he was a creep.
Do you know that I have never understood what they meant
by "grassy knoll." It sounds so idyllic, a place to go
to dream your life away, not kill somebody. They
should have called it something like "the grudging notch."
But I guess that's life. What is it they always say?
"It's always the sweetest ones that break your heart."
You getting hungry yet, hon? I am. When I was seven
I sat in our field and ate an entire eggplant
right off the vine. Dad loves to tell that story,

but I still can't eat eggplant. He says I'll be the first
woman President, it'd be a waste since I talk so much.
Which do you think the fixtures are in the bathroom
at the White House, gold or brass? It'd be okay with me
if they were just brass. Honey, can we stop soon?
I really hate to say it but I need a lady's room.

Memo to the Dark Angel

Mousia, the clock is still
and I circle your breasts like a beggar.
Like a violet-colored colt I'm nipping
at the faint herbage of your soigné lipstick.
Shades of railway arches are chiseling messages
across the very sod I whipsaw on. . . . I am yours
until the cockcrow, until the chants begin.

Plume. Dam. Tangled. Copse, listen to me:
one more grimace of Pernod. The inhabitants,
mostly pickpockets, have contributed heaving
teeter-totters for the victims of insomnia.
Cups of tea and slices of toast are left
for the sharpshooter to see,
and grandchildren are groomed for the festival.

Mousia, resistance. Mousia, please respond now
that I sway in chains, now that I have inherited
this jerking, bobbing leverage, and the grass-blades
imperceptibly graze on the pinto beans. Mousia,
your silken forelock and corridor-eyes, your stamping,
tossing bronchitis I kneel before, your imprisoned
penny's worth of terrain I name catastrophe.

If It Would All Please Hurry

I have escaped from the two-acre rolled garden
where twenty-five fair Anglo-Irish are
consuming champagne. The gnats, I said,
are quite sending me mad. I hope
you will not think it rude
if I go indoors. In fact,
they were eating me fast.
And those terrible smiles
were eating me too.
They smile but cannot laugh.

I am so sleepy and I do not wish
to share the cliffs with anyone
                *
Today I walked up the hill
where they are harvesting the corn,
and right up among the sheep, silly as ever,
to the very top. Underneath
a creaking beech tree I
blew a lot of thistledown
and admired the different golds
of the cornfield,
and came down again.

There is, for once, so little to say.
I cannot go anywhere, start anything now.
Even the bed seems far away
and I am on it.
                *
In the window which looks out onto the limes
there is an unbalanced construction
of colored plastic squares,
it quite takes one's mind off

those enormous trees. Of course
they are marvelous trees,
among the finest in the land,
but trees round a house
are really a mistake:
don't they take the oxygen or something?
They get you somehow.
The trees, and probably the flowers, get you
long before the water.

Pigeons are flopping about
and the Irish are out on their bicycles.
It is going by so quickly
and the sun is falling behind
that unnecessary bush to the right.

*

I am sitting here about to get into this bed
and nearly fall out because every night
I feel you are in it too, and in front of me
is the shepherd boy under his glass tree
with his faithful glass dog
and his woolly glass sheep.
I sleep with a Braun electric fan heater
because of being cold I put it in my bed
it just burns bits. So now I am going
to sleep holding you most tight please
tell me where you are.

I do not like not knowing.

*

Dreamless sleep.
Wake to the usual gloom and forebodings.
If I am some sort of nut who spends life
elaborately avoiding what I like best,
let it be clear.

And I cannot move.
Deep down I feel instinctively I never will.
I cannot *bear* to hurt.
I want to say *don't trust me,*
don't love me, I am hell.

*

On a foggy morning
outside Golders Green cemetery
a cousin is being committed to the flames.
They slide the box slowly, contrivedly, out of sight.
Then words of dull intonation from a man
who never knew the lady,
the little gilt automatic doors.

Beastly cheap tear-jerking movie scene.

I'd like an elaborate service with lots of music
and heaps of prayers just read one after another.

I am hugging you. I am trying
to get into the habit of realizing
you are real.

*

The telephone warbles and chirps out with someone
I don't know who knows someone who
is writing a book around the corner
and wants a cup of tea so I should go
and put the kettle on for heaven knows
how manyeth time my darling love
are you all right you cannot be alone.

I am feeling very dopey probably not eating
better have an egg or several
I must have drunk twenty cups of tea today
and I feel like a teapot, an old stained one.

What is that incantation I used to mutter as a child,
". . . the terrors and dangers of the night . . ."?
It must be a prayer, and kept me awake hours
waiting to glimpse the terrors and dangers
and watch them being warded off, wondering about
the dreadful life grown-ups must lead
to make up a prayer like that.

Hold tight, squeeze.

Interruptions

I long for some, even
one would be a beginning,
not this long flat stretch
of just me and my improvising
of waste, of a kind of heroic
negligence that life does not
appreciate. My loved one
is wobbling—O crème de menthe!
See, I am making my own
interference, jerked stratagem—
her overcoat, my cottage.
Why are we so bad? I hear them
faintly knocking, neutral ducks,
and I am reprimanded.
I am thinking "scalloped potatoes"
are of absolutely no use.
I'm thumping my canteen
and pointing at my nose.
Yes, I lied about "her,"
there wasn't one, but for
that moment a gourd drifted
down the chimney on the pretext
of weeding a peninsula
and nourishing the articulation
of a single bud. Am I forgiven?
Forgotten? This is the constellation
of my own bewilderment. Please,
someone interrupt me.
Hence, whatever, reverts.

Bluebird Houses

What remained of the Army
trotted about the storage rooms
cursing and stammering.
Two squat sergeants were conniving
to knit lapwarmers for their hearts.
The clacking mob outside inhaled,
then blew the petals from their capes:
The new moon was tufted with buzzard down!
A captain sat down to write his wife:
"I remain baffled by their coy profiles;
since Tuesday, the youngest soldiers
have been hunched beneath the eaves
like homeless bluebirds, gurgling
in washed-out clumps of disarray.
They dwindle inconclusively
next to the charred bosom of war.
I am immensely well, will not
be home for Easter, please give my love—
whiff, wilt and laden—to the birds."

To Fuzzy

I was standing outside this cocktail bar, see, on the Nile,
when along came this chick with whom I had passed the
    morning
in the poolhall: We found we shared a deep interest in
    thaumaturgy
as she stroked the 8-ball into the side pocket. Fuzzy Wuzzy,

for that was her name. Probability was her strong suit.
She was a gold mine on the skids, and I yearned to wangle
a weekend with her. I bluffed, "The farther you get away
    from me
the suddener you'll be back." Rotten and lazy, I carried a gun.

I began shrugging toward her, closer, until she turned to ice.
"Since when did you escape from mud," she said, and I
    considered
my predicament, I took time for reflection. "Fuzzy Wuzzy," I
said, "you learned the dark arts through a prolonged sojourn

among myriads of bats nesting in abandoned mines, I know that.
Still, as Nietzsche says, 'Man has regarded his natural
    propensities
with an *evil eye* for too long.' It is not that I wish you
to visit depravities upon me, I would perish first!"

One of the big Pharaohs once told me in a dream that one day
    I would
be very thin and sit in a soft armchair. I would be reading a
    letter,
written in Chinese calligraphy, in pencil, scribbled hastily,
and its central motif would be the mat the author was sitting on

and the writing pencil with which his hand and arm, torso and
  brain
and a lifetime of witnessing, were struggling. I know there are
contradictions in all that I say. Fuzzy, whence is the unseen
vindicated? Esteemed cocktail bar, the Pharaohs have
  edged your

needs into retreat.

Poem to Some of My Recent Poems

My beloved little billiard balls,
my polite mongrels, edible patriotic plums,
you owe your beauty to your mother, who
resembled a cyclindrical corned beef
with all the trimmings, may God rest
her forsaken soul, for it is all of us
she forsook; and I shall never forget
her sputtering embers, and then the little mound.
Yes, my little rum runners, she had defective
tear ducts and could weep only iced tea.
She had petticoats beneath her eyelids.
And in her last years she found ball bearings
in her beehive puddings, she swore allegiance
to Abyssinia. What should I have done?
I played the piano and scrambled eggs.
I had to navigate carefully around her brain's
avalanche lest even a decent finale be forfeited.
And her beauty still evermore. You see,
as she was dying, I led each of you to her side,
one by one she scorched you with her radiance.
And she is ever with us in our acetylene leisure.
But you are beautiful, and I, a slave to a heap of cinders.

A Jangling Yarn

Anonymous captive of the pensive habit,
drowsy in my spool of soda,
dank husk of neglected choruses,
I hear the footsteps of the postman
a thousand miles away: He speaks
of trifles, and is often, by his own admission,
unemployed. I am spying on his bloodstream

as a can of darkness pours over my head.
I'm hostile in baggy trousers.
O minuscule thermometer, naked bulb of pain,
I suffocate in your embrace.
Upheaval of chaste embroidery,
I fear your insignificance
and this reminder of what's to come.

Pangs and tears, I tend, I spoon,
and tears tend to make me lose interest.
My landlady, with toothpicks in tune,
sweeps this alarming leaf into her gutter,
her waist crumbling in large blocks,
which a hired truck will collect later.
What further news from the world? Winking,

hissing, creaking, you, grimace, you, sheave
of scissoring cadenzas. I must wake now
into masquerade and particle, act out
my fluffy monologue behind the parrot green
tapestry, lisp some sparkling caprice:
It is Carnival again in the world, and I must try
to harmonize with its proud or shabby downfall.

Paint 'Til You Faint

House, house, go away, you're looking
prettier all the time and look me
I'm a rag, a brush, a mop, a hammer.
I'm your lowly employee not what I intended—
I wanted shelter, a self-propelled houseboat.

Housepainting for a fortnight now,
I have no idea how long I've been stroking
white up down back forth when I
slapped a good juicy one across my face—
I can't get mad at a fool like that.

I kept painting as if nothing happened,
I was in a hurry to get to the fine work
so I painted an ant and then I wrote my name
across the forehead of a flea—
anything domestic like this truly enervates me.

Cash-monster, Time-monster, Thought-police.
I keep painting, I would paint the milkman
but he is already painted. I'd like to get
my brush inside that mole-hole—the boob
who sold me this bill of goods.

The neighbors have witnessed my devotion
to this busted cesspool of a castle, and now
I am a deacon in the Church of their values—
silently, silently, we have painted ourselves
into this little plot of earth.

But now I'd like to paint something more abstract
like Love or Death or Despair, paint
checkerboards on the idly curious, brand them.
Soon enough this cloud will have to be
torn apart and patched and then painted again.

My arms weigh about three tons, spaghetti legs.
Suddenly I feel drawn back to the ocean floor,
which never needs painting. There
I'd plop my head on a hungry mollusk—
adroit chiliastic sub rosa luffing. . . .

Adroit: dexterous in the use of the hands
or in the exercise of the mental faculties;
ready in invention or execution.

Chiliastic: the belief in Christ's return to earth
to reign during the millennium.

Sub rosa: under the rose; covertly; privately; confidentially.

Luffing: sailing a ship closer to the wind.

Tragedy's Greatest Hits

I remember the puddles and tensions, I see
the cruel boats thrashing against the gate.
I couldn't resist floating there before
the chime of meekly barking fetters.
I took the silence and snapped it,
and forgot remembered forgot.
The King stood there shivering,
soaked to the bone.

He coughed at the crowd: The big guy
was harmless now. How torrid to magnify
this cloudy downfall! At the axis, however,
there was something tantalizing, a few
gunshots and a morbid rambling.
One, a hooker, called him "Honey,"
and got away with it.

In a limbo of sad, soft crowns, a line
was about to be lost between us.
His power was blurring, he whose glance
could kill, whose snout yesterday
could fling dread, now dripped,
and the rabble whistled and relished
every drop of it.

I was the stuttering monster who accepted
his doom. But he was coasting
on the past.

Life moves on, where are the miracles?

It's twelve o'clock, I wish
it were eleven-fifty-nine.

Toward Saint Looey

I was talcuming my windshield
below the basalt slabs on our dead-end street.
The chrome crackled within earshot of the pines.
My big glittering black eyes snagged
on a small derisive spume of dust—
he who in shapes makes visible—
and I thought back on the bliss of the many,
the oval radiances of my bony knees.
Blackmailer, nicest smile, false move.

In the rear-view mirror I was dozing,
knifefishes played among the weeds.
A huge stag beetle brought me cookies.
Take me back to Saint Looey, sideways,
and give me a silver dollar
dredged from the murky green water,
the life-stream, the blood,
at-one-ment in a glorious blue light.
I brake, skidding, the steering wheel

thrashing like an eel, almost edible.
The brother of the left-hand path, also known
as Eddie, twinkled out of Chiseltown
to nest beside me in the final stage.
Now this was palpable, his blood bright,
past the small warts and radar aerials
like anesthesia in a circular route
we sped. Orientation reflexes deviating
from our landmark destination, the smoking dog.

We devoured our prey; little one, is it
memory again? Whippets scattered into the hedges,
and the road turned to gravel as we churned

up the steep last hill. A pigeon leered
before we scattered him. Transmuted,
desireless, thud. "Get the ice bucket, Eddie,
things are beginning to evaporate,
we are at the threshold, the stone wall."
I could sense the carport, the aggregate of feelings,

the path our teachers took, just ahead
in the fawn-colored afternoon, suspended
above the smug charities, in the vicinity
of the screwy briefcases and narrower caves.
We were thrusting our way into the actual
storage batteries, hunching toward canary-yellow.

Earthworks

A thin covering of sickly grass.
The coffee plantation, atrophied. No trophies.
The town clerk with his papery mortgages (in his
desk drawer a mouse fingers the testimonials).
Or the dish well-nigh balanced by the cornfield,
near the corn-belt, that was habitually empty?
Is there a remedy? Equipment should be arriving soon

to remove the icebergs from the Barrens, the pebbles
along with flakes of snow into the further seams.
Lawsuits will be melting next to the Grand Design.
Felled trunks and uprooted families leave spittle
at the base of the new towers. There has arisen
a new, disorderly vegetation between patches of
dead ground. Whereas, the original character

of the mountain-world was a ballet of mineral witnesses
before the manifest herbal presence of, say, marjoram.
A survey shows the sky was undependable.
Oh well, you can't look back. You can, but—
a wretched entanglement of half-hearted trees—
no company ever went from them unthankful—
a scent, a drizzle, the disgarnished plateau.

On the World's Birthday

There's so much good in a face, such hope!
If I pulled all of these daggers out of my forehead
could I breathe like a jet in an exemplary way,
like a bean?

I belong to a special section of the Gnat Squad,
we are quite busy just now trying to convince ourselves
that ours is the most special squad
(what a yawn on stilts!).

The theory of fusion has fallen short, it's over-
dark victory. If only I were allowed to say,
then it is your recovery that counts . . .
Bunny!

And I will go along with you just this far:
He forgot his hat. Happy, happy,
I mean really a knocked-out feather,
that sharing,

that love-disease and courtly fear,
that erasure that nearly reaches you
stops and tilts toward other worlds
and the tiny hour of two.

IX

from Reckoner

(1 9 8 6)

Jo Jo's Fireworks—Next Exit

Past the turpentine camps,
brilliant green lamps held
by woozy militiamen,
the car with a nose of its own,
with headlight-eyes, sniffs
through the mountain fog,
heart palpitating, belly
hungry for gasoline pancakes.
Ghettos rave in their sleep,
butchering alto solos,
harvesting white snakes.
The car, evermore threadbare,
feels lost on Chevrolet Avenue,
a victim of the Taxi Wars.
Salamanders glow like tiny cutlets
and each Inn is in secret
a detention barracks, each
exit an entrance to underground
cuniculi, concatenation
of clandestine suburbs
from which there is no escape
until dawn, when bellboys are young.

No Rest for the Gambler

I am sitting quietly on the verandah, an instrument
for the composition of replies is smoking next to me,
a decoy with a frown.

These are the kinds of details that exhaust me—pine
needles, a fly in a web, seashells—the details
you can never forget for noticing—Sophia's slowly

gliding ducks, her cleavage, her gum. . . . I have questions
that take the form of whippings with fronds, of idleness,
unhappy ancestors fanning the dawn. I predict the destruction

of the temples of Hucumba, and the election of Slick Jones.
Something once terribly important has been lost,
like an island, an embroidered blouse, a colleague

in the parallel world. A swindler's victory, a fly
I had once known. I disapprove, I don't remember!
Beyond the reef are sharks and the dainty frippery

of childhood, and, once there, there is no filching.
I was premature on the beach, like algae at lunchtime
sleepwalking with a harp proscribed by hawks.

One looks backward and one looks forward.
Dust is watching life's talk show.
I plunge like danger into the sea.

My mother stands, facing the wind.

A Wedding

She was in terrible pain the whole day,
as she had been for months: a slipped disc,
and there is nothing more painful. She

herself was a nurse's aide, also a poet
just beginning to make a name for her
nom de plume. As with most things in life,

it happened when she was changing channels
on her television. The lucky man, on the other
hand, was smiling for the first time

in his life, and it was fake. He was
an aspiring philosopher of dubious potential,
very serious, but somehow lacking in

essential depth. He could have been
an adequate undertaker. It was not the first
time for either of them. It was a civil

service, with no music, few flowers.
Still, there was a slow and erratic tide
of champagne—corks shot clear into the trees.

And flashcubes, instant photos, some blurred
and some too revealing, cake slices that aren't
what they were meant to be. The bride slept

through much of it, and never did we figure out
who was on whose team. I think the groom
meant it in the end when he said, "We never

thought anyone would come." We were not the first
to arrive, nor the last to leave. Who knows,
it may all turn out for the best. And who

really cares about such special days, they
are not what we live for.

The List of Famous Hats

Napoleon's hat is an obvious choice I guess to list as a famous hat, but that's not the hat I have in mind. That was his hat for show. I am thinking of his private bathing cap, which in all honesty wasn't much different than the one any jerk might buy at a corner drugstore now, except for two minor eccentricities. The first one isn't even funny: Simply it was a white rubber bathing cap, but too small. Napoleon led such a hectic life ever since his childhood, even farther back than that, that he never had a chance to buy a new bathing cap and still as a grown-up—well, he didn't really grow that much, but his head did: He was a pinhead at birth, and he used, until his death really, the same little tiny bathing cap that he was born in, and this meant that later it was very painful to him and gave him many headaches, as if he needed more. So, he had to vaseline his skull like crazy to even get the thing on. The second eccentricity was that it was a *tricorn* bathing cap. Scholars like to make a lot out of this, and it would be easy to do. My theory is simple-minded to be sure: that beneath his public head there was another head and it was a pyramid or something.

Jelka Revisited

Jelka's profile decorates the doorway to my secret architecture.
Jelka's profile chaffs at its own imposture, and the indirection
of its stardust infiltrates my polar brain: Welcome
to the material world where omens of the afterworld are
    leaked,
flowing like a black shirt. Mountains migrate into my head:
I was there to witness the vulgar radiance of her method,
dimly brooding under my Western lamp, accustomed, as I am,
to a miscellany of risible phantasms, fatigue never set in.
"Pungent nit, come in! Comfort my belligerent lashes, help me
cast out my throes." Jelka's profile, O the asymmetry of it all!
She staggers now, and attempts to install a puzzle in her smile.
To the tune of Gylfi's mocking, this goddess of illusion
I shall never forget: all living is forgiving. Her profile.

Within Jelka's radius, a Colonel is pulling a thorn
from a comrade's melancholy frown.
There is undischarged thunder in the air. Skeptical,
Jelka looks around, spots a mathematician
playing marbles in the darkened parlor.
Several travelers appear indisposed and refuse
an offer of dinner. Jelka is stimulated
by these companions and walks around
feeling pregnant. Was Hirshvogel going North
or South? "Go after him when you are bigger,"
said the neighbor. The buttons, the buttonholes,
silver heels—brooch which consists of single
flaming beryl—whisk broom, please, carhop. The fête
by the tomb was a horrible idea. Jelka's tongue
felt like suede. Her slippers, too, were antique, blessed things
making sure she "never fell off Mister Floor."

Thirty olive trees are scribbling with crayons
on the bowler hats of eagles—ah, the train!

Jelka snatched up the idle boy, the viscous child saint,
and cuddled him all the way to Illinois.
Wanderers. Whoosh, their luggage. They stand there,
pigheaded in Poisonville, bleeding lemonade
onto the drip-dry tarmac. They are traveling
under pseudonyms, their whole lives flickering
in corridors. Around five, the bonfires,
and they come whipcracking out of their comas.
Lynxes are burrowing into their sleep-filled wagons.
And the boy with the mark of the beast . . . his
transitory gleam and headlong flight . . . Jelka follows
him flattening her endearments against the linoleum
shadow-stippled in the afternoon.

Jelka was lost forever, her costume found burnt
at daybreak. Could have been the city itself
just having a good time. I wish I knew
its name, brute nebulae. When her Collected Phonecalls
were published last Fall, she didn't remember
making any of them. So. American roués.
She was a ghost at her own birthday party.
"Look at her," said the Colonel, "she twiddles the dust-babies,
baleful and bluish, with fewer fingernails to grow.
Her life swings back and forth like a tongueless bell,
so far from anyone's home." I wrung his neck, and now
all of that old world is torn down. A coach arrives
to take her back to her inkspot, her comfortable
decomposing zones.

Smart and Final Iris

Pentagon code
for end of world
is *rural paradise,*
if plan fails
it's *rural paradise*

For losses under
100 million, *a trip
on the wayward bus*

For a future of mutants,
bridal parties collide

World famine is
a plague of beatniks

First strike and
I sniff your nieces
   I fall to pieces
      Get hell out . . .

A madman comes,
one of those babies
the further you kick it
the bigger it gets.

The Chaste Stranger

All the sexually active people in Westport
look so clean and certain, I wonder
if they're dead. Their lives are tennis
without end, the avocado-green Mercedes
waiting calm as you please. Perhaps it is
my brain that is unplugged, and these
shadow-people don't know how to drink
martinis anymore. They are suddenly and
mysteriously not in the least interested
in fornicating with strangers. Well,
there are a lot of unanswered questions
here, and certainly no dinner invitations
where a fella could probe Buffy's inner-
mush, a really complicated adventure,
in a 1930ish train station, outlandish
bouquets, a poisonous insect found
burrowing its way through the walls
of the special restaurant and into one
of her perfect nostrils—she was reading
Meetings with Remarkable Men, needing
succor, dreaming of a village near Bosnia,
when a clattering of carts broke her thoughts—
"Those billy goats and piglets, they are
all so ephemeral . . ." But now, in Westport
Connecticut, a boy, a young man really,
looking as if he had just come through
a carwash, and dressed for the kind of success
that made her girlfriends froth and lather,
can be overheard speaking to no one
in particular: "That *Paris Review* crowd,
I couldn't tell if they were bright or
just overbred." Whereupon Buffy swings
into action, pinning him to the floor:
"I will unglue your very being from this

planet, if ever . . ." He could appreciate
her sincerity, not to mention her spiffy togs.
Didymus the Blind has put three dollars
on Total Departure, and I am tired of pumping
my own gas. I'm Lewis your aluminum man, and
we are whirling in a spangled frenzy toward
a riddle and a doom—here's looking up

your old address.

Ash Manor

The ghost said nothing that added to our knowledge
of the current situation at Ash Manor, only, as he parted,
"Your flesh would make delicious veal chops
for hungry wolves." Then he called us his "disciples."

Like the slow emigration of the mad, in the half-silence,
I blew upon the lock of the door and it opened.
I blew upon the candle, which lit itself. It was not
a dream—it was a puzzle. In my mouth there was a bowl

of beef stew, but I could not eat it. I felt hungry,
but it was not really hunger, only a feeling of hunger.
Though, fortunately, observations on bees living in the tropics
have thrown a little light on the question: as if I had

bitten my throat with my own teeth. Nevertheless the waves
of the primeval Ocean of Tantalassa were swashing over
pet seals, Tex and Tulip. A Cult was immediately formed
whose solemn purpose it was to design new uniforms for the
     servants.

Here was a sad emotion, belonging exclusively to the sphere
of civilized man. Photographs were taken of a trumpet
in the air; a rebuke, it nested there long after sunset,
in darkness. My eyes moistened, my great burning eyes.

The dwarfs on my side were like myself, only much shorter
and black. The dwarfs on the other side were real dwarfs,
who were really six feet tall like myself, or even eight feet tall,
but they looked as if they were no bigger than a child.

I have a little dog and they want to take him away from me.

Machines are being installed in my head.

A Vagabond

A vagabond is a newcomer
in a heap of trouble.
He's an eyeball at a peephole
that should be electrocuted.
He's a leper in a textile mill
and likely to be beheaded, I mean,
given a liverwurst sandwich
on the break by the brook
where the loaves are sliced.
But he oughtn't meddle
with the powder puffs on the golf links—
they have their own goats to tame,
dirigibles to situate.
He can act like an imbecile
if the climate is propitious,
a magnate of kidnap
paradising around the oily depot,
or a speck from a distant nebula
wishing to purchase a certain skyscraper. . . .

Well, if it's permitted, then
let's regulate him, let's testify
against his thimble, and moderate his gloves
before they sew an apron.

The local minister is thinking
of moving to Holland, exchanging
his old ballads for some lingerie.
"Zatso!" says the vagabond.
Homeless, like wheat that tattletales
on the sermon, like wages swigged.
"Zatso, zatso, zatso!" cries the vagabond.
The minister reels under the weight
of his thumbs, the vagabond seems to have

jutted into his kernel, disturbed
his terminal core. Slowly, and with
trifling dignity, the minister removes
from his lapel his last campaign button:
Don't Mess with Raymond, New Hampshire.

Neighbors

Will they have children? Will they have more children?
Exactly what is their position on dogs? Large or small?
Chained or running free? Is the wife smarter than the man?
Is she older? Will this cause problems down the line?
Will he be promoted? If not, will this cause marital stress?
Does his family approve of her, and vice versa? How do
they handle the whole inlaw situation? Is it causing some
discord already? If she goes back to work, can he fix
his own dinner? Is his endless working about the yard
and puttering with rain gutters really just a pretext
for avoiding the problems inside the house? Do they still
have sex? Do they satisfy one another? Would he like to
have more, would she? Can they talk about their problems?
In their most private fantasies, how would each of them
change their lives? And what do they think of us, as neighbors,
as people? They are certainly cordial to us, painfully
polite when we chance-encounter one another at the roadside
mailboxes—but then, like opposite magnets, we lunge
   backward,
back into our own deep root systems, darkness and lust
strangling any living thing to quench our thirst and nourish
our helplessly solitary lives. And we love our neighborhood
for giving us this precious opportunity, and we love our dogs,
our children, our husbands and wives. It's just all so damned
difficult!

The Sadness of My Neighbors

Somehow, one expects
all that food
to rise up
out of the canning jars
and off the dinner plates
and *do* something,
mean something.

But, alas, it's all
just stuff and more
stuff, without pausing
for an interval
of transformation.

Even family
relationships
go begging
for any illumination.

And yet, there is competence,
there is some quiet
glitter to the surface,
a certain cleanliness,
which means next to

nothing, unless you want
to eat off the floor.

Thoughts While Reading
The Sand Reckoner

What nourishes the polar star?
That's a story I refuse to tell.
Bellhops lacking a pineapple?
Or the secret ingredients of bubblebath?
Itself a derailed story. And still
stuntmen by the school are washed ashore.
What would be inappropriate here is deep-
fried calamaries, or the sound of a crossbow
humming. I have been reading for hours,
I am counting every little grain of sand.
Saturday night in Amherst: Archimedes is my man.
I drift toward nightfall, renaming all
the recent immigrants from Antarctica.
("We shall have a good voyage if God is willing.")
Disconsolate bunglers, incalculable cloves,
the Ship sang. Ginger scurvy.
Then I took one of them around to see chlorophyll
working in the meadow, and later bought him
a porkpie hat. Night was coming on, hell,
night had come and gone and I was still
reading, reading my way through the library.
Night had come and gone leaving not a trace
except me, and I by necessity had moved on
and was by now reading *Magellan's Voyage,*
a Narrative Account of the first Circum-
navigation by Antonio Pigafetta. Poor mad
Ferdinand died spectacularly at the hands
of Filipino warriors. Seventeen hundred
years before a fellow named Eratosthenes
calculated the circumference of the earth
to be 24,650 miles—not a bad guess, only
two-hundred and twenty-five off. Well,
I was reading about all these stargazers
and felt this aching desire for a newer world

when *Adventures of a Red Sea Smuggler*
tumbled off the shelf. I love Henry de Monfreid
for writing, "I went to see the pyramids.
What a disappointment they were to me. . . ."
His reason: the majesty of the desert
could not be obscured.

Sunday morning in Amherst, I have spotted
a water buffalo! Emily Dickinson
has decided to purchase several mohair jackets,
but it is Sunday and I regret to report
she has not been a very good neighbor lately.
"Tears are my angels now," she said to me
around 4 A.M. "But are they interested
in Cedar Rapids?" I asked. "I'm not qualified
to say," was her sorry reply. And so it went,
the sound of a crossbow humming, my own
jungle fever. My weary and blossoming Soul
was passed from hand to hand to hand.
I was resting in the center of some huge pageant
when a human standing next to me said:
"There must be more," and set out to find it
against all odds, against the known sum.
And years later, either came back or didn't,
was the biggest fool ever, or shines there
on the horizon, like a newly minted coin of hope.
And those who stayed and mocked, and those
who merely read about it later—the grains
of untrammelled sand fall through their brains
long after the sojourner has begun to snore.

Storm

The snow visits us,
taking little bits of us with it,
to become part of the earth,
an early death and an early return—

like the filing of tax forms.
And all you can say after adding up
column after column: "I'm not myself."

And all you can say after the long night
of searching for one certain scrap of paper:
"It never existed."

And when all the lamps are lit
and the smell of the stew
has followed you upstairs
and slipped under the door of your study:
"The lute is telling the story
of the life I might have lived,
had I not—"

In my study, which is without heat,
in mid-January, in the hills
of a northern province—only
the thin white-haired volumes
of poetry speak, quietly, like
unfed birds on a night visit

to a cat farm. And an airplane is lost
in a storm of fitting pins.
The snow falls, far into the interior.

Stella Maris

There was nothing to do on the island. The dogs chased glass lizards into the dense myrtle bush. I don't know how the children slept. Men and women did what they could to extinguish the brightness of the stars.

One night my own supply of rum ran out, and I paced the verandah of my little hut-on-stilts. A ship was passing, the air was warm and moist like an animal's tongue. The island had once been home to pirates and runaway slaves, and giant sea turtles that crawled out by moonlight to lay their eggs. I no longer remembered what brought me there. And always the sound of the sea, like an overtone of eerie applause, the clapping of the palms of the palmettos.

I was dreaming, slightly intoxicated, and I found myself standing outside the little Catholic church, Stella Maris, "Star of the Sea." The priest stood before me, a beaten, disheveled man with ashes on his robes and the unmistakable aroma of alcohol like an unholy ghost drawing us closer.

"These people," he said, waving his arms around at his imaginary flock, "they think love's easy, something nice and tidy that can be bought, that makes them feel good about themselves. Believe me, it's a horrible thing to love. Love is a *terrible* thing, terrible!"

And I, an unbeliever, believed him. The next day the owner of the liquor store told me that the priest had been a Jew and a lawyer from New York before converting and becoming a priest assigned to this, the dregs of the Pope's Empire. Sharks and wild boar had thinned out the unbelievers. And Father Moser drank through the night, testing his faith with Fyodor Dostoevsky.

I never knew whether or not I had dreamed up that black-hearted priest, but I left the island shortly, and only now look back at my darkest hour with nostalgia.

UNIVERSITY PRESS OF NEW ENGLAND publishes books under its own imprint and is the publisher for Brandeis University Press, Brown University Press, Clark University Press, The University of Connecticut, Dartmouth College, Middlebury College Press, University of New Hampshire, University of Rhode Island, Tufts University, University of Vermont, and Wesleyan University Press.

ABOUT THE AUTHOR   James Tate grew up in Kansas City, Missouri. He is the author of *The Lost Pilot* (1967), *The Oblivion Ha-Ha* (1970), *Hints to Pilgrims* (1971), *Absences* (1972), *Viper Jazz* (1976), *Riven Doggeries* (1979), *Constant Defender* (1983), *Reckoner* (1986), and *Distance from Loved Ones* (1990). He teaches at the University of Massachusetts and lives in Amherst.

Library of Congress Cataloging-in-Publication Data

Tate, James.
    [Poems. Selections]
Selected poems / James Tate. — 1st ed.
    p.   cm. — (Wesleyan poetry)
ISBN 0-8195-2190-6 (alk. paper). — ISBN 0-8195-1192-7 (pbk. : alk. paper)
    I. Title.   II. Series.
PS3570.A8A6   1991
811'.54—dc20
                                                                90-50918
                                                                CIP